David Hill has written more than 50 books for children and young adults over the past three decades. His work has been published all around the world, translated into several languages, and has won awards in New Zealand, the United States, the United Kingdom, France and Germany. In 2021 he was awarded the Prime Minister's Award for Literary Achievement in Fiction. He lives and writes in New Plymouth, New Zealand.

ALSO BY DAVID HILL

Below
Coastwatcher
Finding
Flight Path
Enemy Camp
The Deadly Sky
Brave Company
My Brother's War
Coming Back
The River Runs
No Safe Harbour
See Ya, Simon

STEPPING UP

DAVID HILL

PENGUIN BOOKS

PENGUIN

UK | USA | Canada | Ireland | Australia
India | New Zealand | South Africa | China

Penguin is an imprint of the Penguin Random House group of companies, whose addresses can be found at global.penguinrandomhouse.com

First published by Penguin Random House New Zealand, 2026

Design by Katrina Duncan © Penguin Random House New Zealand
Cover illustration by Phoebe Morris
Author photograph by Robert Cross

Printed and bound in Australia by Griffin Press, an Accredited ISO AS/NZS 14001 Environmental Management Systems Printer

A catalogue record for this book is available from the National Library of New Zealand.

ISBN 978-1-77695-342-4
eISBN 978-1-77695-676-0

Many thanks to:
Dr Rall Koen
Tessa Nation-Ingle, Physiotherapist
Tim Saunders, Clinical Prosthetist

ONE

'Better go on the uphill side of those boulders.' Ben Coles' father pointed. 'Safest way.'

'Be quicker underneath them,' Ben said. 'Shingle looks pretty solid there. Easier to walk on.'

They stood side by side, staring across the fifty . . . sixty metres of gravel and boulders that angled downwards in front of them. On the far side of the slope, bush rose, tall and green and sheltering. They both huddled inside their parkas as another gust of wind moaned past.

When Pangonui last erupted nearly a thousand years ago, lava had come pouring down these slopes. Rocks the size of trucks had been flung from the crater; crashing and bounding downwards. Some had hurtled for hundreds of metres. Others remained sunk in the big black mountain's shingly flanks, like the one Ben could see ahead of them.

Centuries of rain and frost had broken rocks down into the pebbles that covered the slopes. These pebbles were always moving, rolling, trickling across the track that Ben and his father were tramping now. Moving across these shingle slopes was a pain: slipping, sliding, with stones getting inside shoes. The less time you had to spend on them, the better.

The wind moaned again. Ben tucked his chin deeper into his parka collar. 'Let's get moving, Dad. It's freezing here.'

Mr Coles kept standing, eyes scanning ahead. Ben sighed. 'It's freezing!' he went again.

'Follow where I go,' his father replied. 'Try to use my footmarks. It'll be firmer.'

The man moved off, working across the slope, stamping his feet into the crumbly pebbles. Ben followed, using his dad's footprints — yeah, it did make things easier — muttering to himself when Mr Coles paused to check the next few metres. The wind whined once more; seemed to slice straight through his parka. Couldn't his father go any faster? This was snail speed.

He took an impatient stride forward. His foot missed the hollow his dad had stamped and sank into the shingle.

Next minute, his sneaker was full of pebbles. He muttered to himself again, shook his foot, tried to hook out the loose stuff. A couple of bits stayed wedged under his sock. He shook his foot harder, but they wouldn't shift.

The pile of boulders was closer now. Maybe his father was moving at *fit* snail speed? Then Ben groaned as he saw his dad beginning to edge upwards on the slope, so that they would pass above the jumble of big rocks. That would take forever! And look: the ground right underneath the boulders was firm and almost level.

'Hey, Dad!' he called. 'It'll be much easier below the boulders. Quicker, too.'

His father paused, gazed at the jumble of grey-black slabs, shook his head. 'We don't know how stable that stuff is. We're taking the safe route, OK?'

Ben huffed, and didn't care if his dad heard. Those boulders looked like they hadn't shifted in the thousand years they'd lain there. Their great shapes, big as cars, big as buses, even, lay half-buried in the shingle. No way were they going to move just because somebody was walking underneath them.

The wind whined once more. Dust lifted from the shingle and blew against Ben's face, making him screw up his eyes. Five metres ahead, his father was labouring upwards. Ben glanced at him, glanced at the hard stretch of ground below the cram of huge stones. Next minute, he was turning away from his dad's stamped footmarks, angling downwards to pass beneath the boulders, instead of above.

A dozen scrambling, half-sliding steps, and he was nearly level with his father, who still struggled slowly upwards on the slope above. Mr Coles must have glimpsed him; his head jerked around, and he stared. 'What are you —?'

'It's all right!' Ben called. 'It's safe — and faster!' The man started to say something, but another gust of wind drowned him out.

Ten more sliding, crunching paces. Ben was almost down to the boulders now. Man, some of them were huge: as big as *double-decker* buses, nearly. Smaller ones, the size of fridges or microwaves, lay jammed among them.

The strip of ground under the pile was hard and almost level, just like he'd thought. There was hardly any loose shingle, either. He'd be past and heading for the shelter of the trees before his father had even got round the top of the pile.

He half-stepped, half-slid the last couple of metres, and grabbed the nearest boulder. It was chill and grey, pitted with holes where the volcano's gases must have burst out, way back. He smacked it with his palm. Solid as . . . as a rock. Nothing would ever make this shift.

He was even protected from the wind down here. He grinned; stopped for a second to gaze down the flank of the maunga, where it plunged towards the plains below.

Pity Manu couldn't see this. His best mate might be better at soccer than Ben (and at Maths and Science in their Year 10 class), but Ben was The Mountain Man (and better at English and Social Studies).

He took a last look down the steep, grey-black slope. Then he moved on, easily and steadily along the almost level ground beneath the bulking grey stones.

Twenty metres, and he'd nearly reached the end. The hard ground changed to shingle again; he gripped the boulder he was passing under, so he didn't slide down and get another lot of annoying stones inside his sneakers.

One more boulder to get around. Two, actually, with a gap dividing them, table-sized chunks of rock jammed between. The ground had fallen away beneath these two; he'd have to hold on to them, and swing himself past. No problem: he'd still be miles ahead of his father.

Ben stretched for the corner of the far slab. It was just out of reach. He grunted; grasped one of the rocks jammed into the gap, began hauling himself forward. One swing, and he'd be —

The rock he was gripping made a graunching noise and shifted. He heard the grinding of stone on stone. He lurched, losing his balance, still clinging to the pitted black surface.

Another scraping and graunching. A shape the size of a refrigerator seemed to rise up on end above him, darkening the sky. Ben tried to throw himself forward, but his left foot skidded in the shingle. He fell sideways, leg doubled up beneath him. Next second, something slammed into his body, driving every bit of breath from him, smashing him face downwards onto the stony ground.

TWO

Ben was sprawled on his front, shoved face-down into the shingle. There was blood in his mouth; he could feel and taste the salt of it. He hadn't broken some teeth, had he? He'd have to go to the dentist, and he hated even getting a clean and polish. He ran his tongue around his mouth. Was that a gap at the front there? Aw, hell! Just imagine the smart-arse things Manu and Connor would say.

He tried to turn over and sit up, but his body wouldn't move. Something was holding him down. That boulder: he remembered it now. His legs weren't hurting; they felt heavy and numb, but no pain. He tried to turn again, but he was completely stuck.

'Ben! Ben!' He heard his father shouting; tried to

call back, but his voice came out clogged and croaky. He wriggled his face sideways in the dust and gravel; felt something scrape across his lips. Maybe they were cut; that must be where the blood was coming from.

A scraping, slithering sound. Another boulder toppling! No, his father, skidding to a stop beside him, crouching down and staring. 'Ben! Son! You OK?'

My face, Ben tried to say. *Is it . . . ?* He struggled once more to sit or turn over, managed to get a hand up beside his head, but the rest of his body wouldn't move.

'Stay still!' his father panted. 'That boulder's right across you. You don't — oh, Christ!'

It's OK, Ben wanted to say. *It doesn't hurt; must have just pushed me down into the shingle. But my face . . .* He swallowed, went 'Da—'. But the rocks, the blood in his mouth, the wind whining past and blowing more dust into his eyes were all going blurry and dark. Everything was fading.

He was home in bed. He could feel the warm duvet under his cheek. His father was shouting something at him. 'Up . . . Quickly!' *It's too early*, Ben tried to say, but his tongue felt thick and dry.

Then he saw his dad, a couple of metres away, talking on his phone. The man stood hunched over, shivering in his shirtsleeves. At the same time, Ben realised the duvet under his cheek was his father's jumper, which he must have pushed there. Something else covered his shoulders. His dad's parka.

'Up on the shingle slopes!' Mr Coles was half-yelling into the phone. 'Quickly! . . . What? . . . He can't! There's a boulder on top of him!'

It's all right, Dad, Ben wanted to say. *As long as I don't have to go to the dentist.* He thought out the words, opened his sore mouth to say them, made another croaking sound instead. Next second, his father was kneeling beside him again, one hand on his son's shoulder. 'It's all right, mate. Don't try and move. They'll be here soon!' His dad panted; his eyes stared.

Aw no, they're not sending a dentist up here, are they? Ben wondered. That'll really suck. He tried to tell his father, but the world was going dark at the corners once again.

WHOMP! WHOMP! WHOMP! What was that? The dentist hadn't brought a drill up with him, had he?

Ben tried to jerk his head away, felt the jersey under his cheek, saw the pebbles in front of his eyes.

His father was talking again, on the phone. Not his father: another man. Ben managed to turn his head a fraction, saw someone dressed all in orange handing a yellow parka to his shivering dad. Behind them, another person was somehow sliding down out of the sky. He reached the ground, undid something around his waist, and Ben glimpsed a cable snaking up into the air. *WHOMP! WHOMP!* The noise kept on; then it seemed to grow more distant.

He heard panting and gasping sounds, knew something was happening down by his legs. 'Can't — lift it,' a voice grunted. 'Have to dig.'

Different noises: something metal crunching into the shingle, over and over. His father knelt beside him again, murmuring 'Hold on, son. You'll be OK. Just hold on.'

No worries, Ben wanted to tell him once more. *As long as my teeth . . .* The crunching sound stopped. A voice grunted 'Slowly. Really slowly', and he knew the bottom half of his body was being shifted sideways. It felt heavy and thick. No wonder, being stuck under the boulder all that time. Now he could sit up and ask —

His father moved instead; lurched backwards and made a choking sound. 'His leg —'

'Easy, mate.' One of the other voices. 'Looks bad with all the dirt and stuff. We'll put him on the chopper. Let's just get him ready first.'

A different face appeared in front of Ben. The man in orange. He had a beard, looked a bit younger than Ben's dad. He held a white box. 'Hello there, buddy. Been trying a bit of boulder-surfing, eh? We've got you now. Gonna give you something so you're comfortable.'

A tugging feeling near his shoulder. *Snip, snip*: the sleeve of his parka was being cut open. And his jumper and shirt underneath. *Oh, no, Mum is going to be seriously not pleased about this*, Ben knew. He tried to say so to the bearded figure, who was getting something out of the white box. Then something pricked at his right arm.

'Parka,' he whispered; heard it come out as '*—ark*'.

'Just lie still, son.' That was his father, crouching beside the other man. *WHOMP! WHOMP!* The sound was growing again. No, it was going away. Everything felt . . .

Now he was dreaming. He must be, because he was floating up into the sky, lying warm and comfortable on a bed. Even his mouth had stopped hurting.

WHOMP! WHOMP! Louder once more. Ben blinked; stared up. A big orange shape hung above him in the air, something spinning and blurring above it. A helicopter. He was going to ride in a helicopter. Awesome!

His bed seemed to swing slowly one way, then the other. The shingle slopes and boulder outcrops of Pangonui drifted past beside him. He could see the track leading into the bush, where he and his father had been heading. *Soon as I've been to the dentist, we'll do the walk again*, he decided. *Oh, and I'll need a new parka.*

WHOMP! WHOMP! He stopped rising. Hands held his bed, began pulling him inside a little space or something. He glimpsed straps being undone, heard a metal door slide shut, and the whomping sound seemed quieter. Another face, no beard this time, peered down at him. 'OK, buddy, we're on our way. There in ten minutes. You take it easy.'

There? Where? And I'm not gonna take it easy, Ben thought. *My first ride in a chopper, so I'm going to watch the view and everything that happens. Just as soon as I blink my eyes to see properly. As soon as I blink my eyes.*

THREE

Yes, here was the helicopter. He could see it plainly. But he was outside now, not inside, and its rotor blades weren't turning. They hadn't put him back down on the mountain, surely?

He was moving. He still lay in that bed — no, it was a wider one, and he could hear wheels, rattling across concrete or something. A person was pushing him. More than one person; they were talking. 'Straight to theatre, Mr Dev said.'

Theatre? What were they taking him to a movie for? He managed to turn his head; saw someone walking beside him, one hand on the bed. The stretcher, it must be. A woman with dark skin and hair. Quite cute. She smiled at him. 'Hello, Ben. I am Hom. The doctor is wanting to take a look at you. Did you enjoy your helicopter ride?'

He closed his eyes for a second, to think of a reply. When he opened them again, he was somewhere with a huge bright light in the ceiling above him. A cool wet cloth was wiping his face. Brilliant. He saw the woman — Hom — nearby. 'They are making you look handsome, like you usually are.'

My teeth, he wanted to ask. But she'd disappeared, and something was going *snip, snip* again. *You've already stuffed up my parka and jumper*, he thought, then realised the snipping was happening down past his waist. 'The left leg,' a voice said. 'Don't move it.' More snips, and he glimpsed someone lifting up his jeans. Well, they had been his jeans; now they were a crumple of sliced, ripped, filthy blue cloth with — was it? — yeah, bloodstains on them. That boulder must have cut his leg.

A terrible thought seized him. Was Hom gonna see him in his undies? What would Connor and Manu say about *that*?

Time passed. Somehow he knew. The light above him changed. Different voices spoke. Once, he ran his tongue slowly and carefully around his teeth, and they all seemed to be there still. 'Cool!' he said, but it came out as '*Goo—*'.

Another face, one with fair hair above it, appeared and smiled. How come all nurses seemed to have nice smiles? 'Just relax, Ben. You're doing fine.'

Yes, he was. His mouth still hurt, but his teeth were definitely there, and that was the main thing. His back felt like someone had dragged him over a heap of shingle. Maybe they had? His right leg ached; his left foot and ankle kept giving stabs. But he was alive and safe, even though he'd been such an idiot. He'd say sorry to his dad. Was *he* all right, too?

More time. A touch on his knee. His right; no, his left knee. A different voice, a man's one, talking: '. . . both tibia and fibula . . . major tissue damage . . . blood vessels . . .'

Someone else beside him. He blinked; tried to see. Words he'd heard before: '. . . make you comfortable'. The same prick in his right arm that he'd felt up on the mountain. They were gonna get him addicted if they weren't careful. Then a soft slide into more darkness, deeper and more silent than any of the ones before.

A long time had passed. Was it the same day? Was it the same *week*? He couldn't tell. He ached all over now: face, back, both legs. Someone was pushing pins into his left foot. He groaned; heard it come out in a squeak, like a little kid's voice. How shaming!

Another fair head appeared. She was quite cute, too: Manu and Connor were gonna be so jealous. 'Hi, Ben. Just lie still if you can. Would you like something to drink?'

He tried to say 'Yes'. It sounded like '*—iss*', but the nurse seemed to understand. A bendy straw slipped into his mouth. 'Take tiny sips. Don't choke.'

Cool sweetness in his mouth. Awesome. He sipped, gasped, sipped again and again. 'You *are* thirsty!' The fair-haired nurse smiled. 'Want some more?'

'Yes.' Ben felt pleased to hear the word come out properly this time. More beautiful sweetness filled his mouth, seemed to flow down into his whole body. He was hungry, too. No, he was starving. He licked his lips; knew they were swollen. 'Bur — burger?'

The nurse stared for a moment, then burst out laughing behind her mask. 'Only a teenage boy would ask for something like that! Not yet, sorry, Ben. Mr Dev will want to have another look at you first.'

Mr Dev. He'd heard that name somewhere. The nurse was still talking; he tried to listen: '. . . move you in bed a little bit; make sure you don't get any pressure sores.' Hands slowly pulled the bed sheets back — yeah, he was under bed sheets. He wasn't in his undies still, was he?

Two . . . three people were shifting his body to one side, lifting his head (oh man, his neck ached, too), and plumping the pillow up. They straightened his legs; seemed to take forever to do that. Ben tried to raise his knees to help, but one of them said, 'It's all right; we'll do that', so he stopped. Pins still stabbed at his left foot. They'd moved up to his shin as well, now. He felt yet another prick in his arm. He didn't want . . . but the soft darkness crept up once more, and he *did* want that.

People went away. He drifted, heard noises by the bed, opened his eyes. His mum was there. His dad, too, wearing different clothes. Great: he must be home already. He licked his lips; worked out how to tell his father he was sorry for stuffing up their tramp. Then he saw his mother was trying to smile at him, but with tears spilling down her cheeks.

He stared for a while. She must be upset about all the

clothes he'd ruined. Parka, jersey, jeans: he'd have to say sorry to her as well. He closed his eyes again, while he thought up the words. When he opened them once more, his parents had gone.

His left foot and shin kept hurting. He remembered that boulder on him, and his dad saying something as the rescue guys dug him out. Then another voice had mentioned tissue, plus a couple more words. Things were all jumbled up in his head.

Hands moved him again. He half-lifted his own head this time, and a voice said 'Good man, Ben'. He felt cool metal under . . . under his bum? A bowl of some sort. The voice said 'loo . . . use this'. Aw, hell! But before he knew it, he felt himself emptying into the bowl. He was gonna die of embarrassment; he just knew he was. He kept his eyes squeezed shut as the bowl was slipped out.

There was murmuring down by the foot of his bed, then everyone went away. He'd meant to ask if they could give him something for his left foot and shin; they were really stabbing all the time now. That boulder must have crashed down on him really hard. Had he dislocated something in his leg? Was it broken, even? If this meant Manu was going to get even better than him at soccer . . .

The next time he opened his eyes, his parents were beside him again. He felt more awake now. Both his legs still hurt, the left one especially, but not quite as much. The sharp pains had turned into dull aches, mostly in his toes.

He moved his head on the pillow, murmured 'Mum?' His mother jerked, seized one of his hands and squeezed it. 'Ben! Oh, Ben darling, are you —' His father was talking, too. 'You're OK, son. You're going to be all right.'

Mrs Coles was trying to smile at him. 'The surgeon says you're doing really well. Everything is . . .' Her voice faltered, and she glanced at Ben's father.

More stabs in Ben's left shin and ankle. The sharp pins were suddenly back, and someone had heated them up. He tried to shift his foot, but it felt heavy and distant. Was there a plaster cast on it?

'My leg hurts,' he managed to say. 'Pins and needles.' Straightaway his father stood, began reaching under the bed sheets on Ben's right side. 'I'll move it. Tell me where it's more comfortable.'

Ben shook his head, and his neck stabbed, also. 'No. The other leg.' His dad stopped; turned to stare at him. 'The left one. It really hurts in the ankle and foot.' Ben hesitated. 'Is it — is it broken?'

A gasping noise from beside him. His mother's whole

body was shaking. His dad kept staring; began to say something, then stopped.

And Ben began to understand what had happened.

FOUR

'I'm so sorry, love.' His mother was holding his hand. She kept trying not to cry, but her shoulders were shaking. Mr Coles had sat down, one arm around her. His free hand rested on Ben's chest.

'Mr Dev — the surgeon; he's been so good — told us. They tried everything to save your leg, but it was . . . it was . . .' His mum shook her head and swiped a hand across her eyes.

'The leg bones were both smashed, son.' Ben's father swallowed, took a breath. 'Not just broken: smashed. And some of the ankle bones. Plus the nerves and arteries were in a bad way as well. And there was so much dirt and stuff in the wounds from the shingle that Mr Dev was worried about infection.'

‘Oh, don’t, Matt! Don’t!’ Ben’s mum was crying harder. Mr Coles held her against him; he was weeping as well.

Inside his head, Ben heard again the words someone had spoken after he’d been taken from the helicopter. ‘*Major tissue damage . . . tibia and fibula.*’ The last words sounded like cats’ names; for a mad second, he thought he was going to laugh.

Silence for a few seconds. There was something Ben had to know. ‘Wh — where?’

His dad stared. ‘On the mountain, son. Under those rocks. Don’t you remem—’

But Mrs Coles had understood. ‘Below your — your knee, darling. Mr Dev said they . . . they saved as much of the leg as they could.’ She stopped speaking; covered her face with her hands.

His parents said things to him, held his hands, stroked his cheek. Ben spoke words, too, but he didn’t know what they were. After a while, only a nurse was in the room. He felt her holding his wrist, moving the bed sheets around him.

Then the room was empty, except for a low light on the wall, and tubes he could glimpse, snaking from a stand down to his leg.

What leg? He was useless now. Yeah, useless. He’d never be able to tramp or play soccer or go anywhere with his mates again. He wouldn't be anyone anymore. He was finished.

More time drifted by. Another metal bowl slid under him; he kept his eyes shut, used it like before. Someone — a guy this time — gave him another sweet drink. Ben swallowed it, but it didn't taste good this time. It tasted like nothing. Everything was nothing now. He'd have to spend his life in a wheelchair. All those things he and his mates were going to do when they left school — travelling overseas; maybe joining a band, with Connor singing and he plus Manu as roadies or something: they were all finished.

Suddenly, he felt so miserable, so hopeless, that he heard himself sob. The nurse or whoever pulled the drink back, said 'Slowly, buddy'. Ben shook his head. It wasn't the drink. It didn't matter what it was. He and everything were useless.

A small, neat man stood beside his bed, with one of the fair-haired nurses. His dark eyes looked tired. 'Hello, Ben. I'm Rajeet Dev. How are you feeling?'

He lifted a hand as Ben began to open his mouth. 'I know — that's the most stupid question in the world. What I mean is, how is the leg? You are feeling pain there?'

'Some. But . . .' Ben swallowed. He could talk better now, and his head didn't feel so woozy. 'I can still feel my toes. And my ankle hurts, like something is stabbing it. Is it really —'

Mr Dev, he was thinking meanwhile. *This is the man who took my leg. Amputated it.* The word stood in his mind for the first time, made his breath catch.

Mr Dev was nodding. 'I'm afraid so. We tried our best, but the bones were crushed. Especially —'

'Tibia and fibula.' At Ben's murmured words, the surgeon raised his eyebrows.

'Well remembered. And there was much danger of infection from all the dirt in your wounds.' He paused. 'I will not lie to you, Ben. We have a great team here in the hospital, and they will do everything they can to help you recover. And you *will* recover; you are young and strong. Plus prostheses — artificial limbs — are amazing things now.' He paused, watched Ben for a moment. 'But it can't be exactly the same. If you wake up, and a shark is somehow exploring your room, two legs will let you run away. If you have to put your prosthesis on, it takes a little longer. But you can always hit the shark with it.'

Ben knew he was meant to smile, but he couldn't. The surgeon waited another second, then said, 'Now we are going to look at your residual limb — the one we operated on. I want to make sure the wound is healing properly. We will be as gentle as we can, but it may hurt when I take off the dressings. Would you like something in case there is pain?'

Ben hesitated, then shook his head. He'd already had enough needles stuck into his arm. Plus the pain . . . the pain might help him forget what had happened.

'We will be very careful,' The surgeon said again. 'Please tell us if it is too much.' He nodded to the nurse, and they both moved towards the foot of the bed. Towards where there was now nothing but emptiness.

FIVE

It took fifteen . . . maybe twenty minutes. His watch and phone must be somewhere, he thought, stupidly. At one moment, there was a sudden rip of agony below his left knee, and he heard himself half-gasp, half-cry out. Mr Dev spoke instantly. 'That was the only place where the dressings were really stuck. Well done, Ben. I'm just going to lift the limb a little, check all around it.'

The limb. He felt hands moving above his left shin. His ankle stabbed once more. They must be wrong; the leg was still there, surely? It had to be the other one.

The surgeon spoke again. 'Very good. The sutures, the stitches, are all in place. The wound looks nice and clean.'

The wound. So many hard words he had to get used to. Ben began to raise himself up in bed, winced as his neck, back and hips all complained. He glimpsed some sort of frame over his left leg. Mr Dev lifted a hand. 'If you want to see what we have done, then wait another couple of days. Everything looks red and raw just now.' The tired dark eyes seemed to smile. 'Some people even want to take a photo, so I like my stitches to look their best.'

He listened to Ben's heart through a stethoscope; took a small probe from the nurse, slid it into Ben's ear, pulled it out and checked it, then nodded. 'As I say, you are a fit and strong boy. No — a young man: perhaps I should call you Mr Coles?' The eyes smiled again. 'You will be seeing lots of experts over the next weeks. They all know things to help you. Your parents want to help in any way they can, too. They have told me. So, your job is to decide right now that you are going to become active and well once more. Will you do that?'

Ben felt tired again. Exhausted. He nodded, just to make the surgeon go. When he was alone again, he lay, feeling his leg (his non-leg) ache and prick. *Active and well*: he'd never be that again, as long as he lived.

His parents were there once more, sitting silently beside his bed. His mother smiled at him and said something, but Ben felt too tired and miserable to reply. He closed his eyes; heard himself start to breathe slowly.

My phone, he thought again. *Do Manu and Connor know what's happened?* He turned his head slightly, to ask his mother, but it wasn't her. It was the dark-haired nurse who'd helped wheel him into the hospital. Hom. He felt pleased to remember her name; tried to say it aloud. It came out as a mumble.

She turned and smiled. 'Hello, Sleeping Beautiful. You've had the good lie-in. I am your physio — your physiotherapist. Lucky I was on emergency duty when you came in, and could get a look at you. We are going to start you moving again, OK?'

Why? Ben wanted to ask. *It's useless. I'm useless.* He must have said something like that out loud, because Hom shook her head.

'You are not useless, Ben. Maybe you feel that way now, but you will never be useless. We can make things better. We begin now. The longer you are lying there, the weaker and stiffer you get. Your heart grows lazy; your kidneys and muscles have the holiday. We do not want this.'

I don't want anything, Ben thought. But Hom was talking to him again. 'You are listening? First, you count for me in sevens. Seven, fourteen, twenty-one. Go.'

What for? He knew he was staring. But he began. His voice mumbled at first, then grew clearer. 'Seven, fourteen, twenty-one, twenty-eight, thirty-five . . . forty-five? No, forty — forty-two.' He was crap at Maths.

The physio nodded. 'Now I wish you to spell "lunch", but backwards.' Ben stared harder. This was crazy. But — 'h . . . c . . . u. Wait: it's h . . . c . . . n . . . u . . . l.'

Hom nodded. 'Your head is good and clear. The drugs have worn off. Now, I wish you to lift your arms above your head. Eight times. Go.'

It's my leg you're supposed to be looking after, Ben thought. But he did what he was told. Then he had to stretch his arms back behind him eight times, then out to the side. He could feel his unused muscles groaning.

He rolled his head from side to side, twelve times. He breathed as deep as he could, fifteen times. Then another ten, holding his breath while Hom counted to five before letting it out. He could feel his body starting to come to life again. Hom was right; he'd been lying there too long.

'Soon we start you doing the leg exercises. In a couple of days, perhaps. We see.

'Now,' The physio went on, 'I wish you to squeeze your bottom.'

Ben froze. 'What?'

Hom laughed. 'I wish you to make the muscles in your bottom go as tight as you can. It helps with your thigh and leg muscles. We need to make them strong.'

This is something I'm definitely not *gonna tell Connor and Manu about*, Ben decided. He tried it: tightening the muscles in his bum; holding it for a couple of seconds, relaxing, then doing it again. Ten . . . twelve times, while the physio counted.

'Good,' Hom told him. 'You rest now. Have lunch. We do this again soon. If this has made you sore, tell a nurse. There is pain relief you can take.'

Ben lay there after she'd gone. He'd felt a bit better for a while; he'd done something, instead of just lying there. But now he was sinking again. Sinking into being nothing.

Two different nurses, a man and a woman, helped him with lunch. Very carefully, they lifted him up in bed, so his back was propped against big pillows. 'Take it slowly,' said the woman. 'You might feel a bit giddy; you've been lying down . . . oh, getting on for six days.'

'Remember, buddy —' The man went. He was big, muscly-looking, with a shaven head. 'Your body is balanced differently now. Top half weighs more than the bottom half. You might find you sway around when you're sitting up. You'll get used to it.'

Ben ate the toasted sandwich, the cheese, part of the orange. He remembered asking that other nurse for a burger. How would he ever be able to go out with his friends for a takeaway again? He dropped the half-eaten orange on his plate; sat staring at the wall.

'You having much pain?' The woman nurse asked. 'We can give you something.' Ben shook his head. His missing leg throbbed and ached, but once again, he almost welcomed the feeling.

The other nurse took his tray away. 'Gonna leave you sitting up for a bit, buddy. Helps with your circulation. Press this —' he placed a button on a cord beside Ben, '— if you need help for anything. It's twenty-four seven service around here.'

'Hello,' The woman said as the door opened again. 'You've got a visitor.' Ben's father had come in.

Mr Coles pulled a chair up beside the bed and took hold of Ben's hand. He hadn't done that since Ben was a little kid. 'Hey, mate. Good to see you sitting up.'

Ben shrugged. 'Your mother wanted to come in,' his dad went on, 'but she just crashed out in the armchair. Hasn't had much rest for the last few days.'

Still Ben said nothing. His father hesitated. 'Something I need to ask you about, son. They — the hospital — want to know what to do with your leg.'

Do with my . . . Ben sat staring at his father. *Are they planning to glue it back on or something?*

'Some people — they want to keep the . . . the part they've lost, bury it at home or somewhere they know. They feel their body is more complete that way. Or . . .' Mr Coles paused again. 'If you prefer, the hospital can have it for medical students when they're training. Or . . . well, they can get rid of it, incinerate it. Mr Dev says to take your time; you don't have to make your mind up yet.'

When he spoke, Ben's voice sounded flat and dull. 'I don't care. They can do what they want.'

Silence in the room. Finally, Mr Coles spoke. 'Son, I'm sorry. It was my fault.'

Ben blinked. What was his father talking about?

'I should have been watching out. I knew you wanted to go that quicker-looking way. Under the rocks. I thought if I went first, you'd follow. I should have kept an eye on things. I'm sorry.' His voice cracked on his last words. He stood up suddenly, turned towards the door, stayed still for a second. Then he sat and took his son's hand again.

'No, Dad.' The words came without Ben having to think. 'You told me. I wanted the easy way. I was a total dick. *I'm* sorry.'

His father gripped his hand harder. Neither of them said anything. Mr Coles stared at the floor. Ben stared at the bed sheets, the bulge where that frame he'd glimpsed must be keeping them off his leg. His non-leg.

'Got this for you,' his dad said. From his pocket, he pulled a sleek black phone. 'Your old one's ruined; got crunched into the shingle. I gave Manu your new number.'

He stood again, rested a palm on his son's cheek. 'I better get back and see if your mum's woken up. She was snoring a bit when I left. We won't tell her that, though — not if we want to live.' He turned towards the door once more. Then — 'We'll walk Pangonui again, buddy. Some time. We'll finish that tramp, OK?'

The door closed behind him. Ben lay, gazing at the ceiling. An ache throbbed in his left ankle. His ankle that must be . . . where? In a hospital freezer or something, along with the rest of his leg, he supposed. He could think about that quite calmly — how weird.

His dad's last words replayed in his mind. *We'll finish that tramp.* He drew in a deep breath, held it like he'd been doing with Hom, let it out slowly. Pain flared in the remaining part of his leg, but he ignored it. Another deep breath. Could he ever manage what his father had said? He had no idea, but he was going to try.

The new black phone lay on his bedside table. *Cool*, he thought, and felt startled. Yeah, he was gonna try. Maybe he wouldn't be totally useless after all.

SIX

He turned on his new phone. Messages: three . . . five . . . heaps of them. Manu first: *Ur super-cool bro / The one u know / sez hello. We all thinking of u. Ur dad sez u on drugs!! Ones to help you get good again. So no visits from us cool dudes in case we got germs. My whānau send luv. C U soon as u get home. We can handle this, bro. We WILL.*

Ben gazed at the wall. For the first time tears came into his eyes. *We*. He wasn't alone; his mates cared, there were so many people ready to help him. Yeah, he was gonna give it his best shot.

More messages, from Connor, other guys in his classes, plus ones he knew from around school. From his Auntie Josie and Uncle Kyle, even his form teacher (and cool English teacher) Mrs Sione. His dad must have given the whole world his new number. He read them all, sent replies to Manu and Connor, then suddenly felt totally exhausted. His left foot (how long till he stopped thinking of it that way?) burned with pain. His shoulders and neck ached. He leaned back against the pillows. He'd rest for a couple of minutes, then text some of the others. Just a couple of minutes.

He jerked awake as Mr Dev arrived in his room with the big shaven-headed nurse. Suddenly, the place was full of movement. The surgeon shone a little torch in his eyes, listened to his heart again, checked whatever it was the nurse had slipped into his ear. 'Your temperature is good. *You* look good. Much pain?'

'A bit. My foot — the one that's not there' (he'd have to think of a better way to say that) '— it hurts sometimes.'

Mr Dev watched him. 'Don't be too brave, Ben. We kept you on painkillers for the first days, and it's good if you don't get dependent on those. But too much pain can slow your healing, so tell us if you want help. I'm going to change your dressings again. Would you like something?'

'I —' Ben shook his head. If he was going to give things his best shot, he'd start now.

'As long as you don't try too much too soon.' Mr Dev seemed almost to be reading his mind. When Ben shook his head again, the surgeon nodded to the big burly nurse. Together, they moved him till he was lying on his back once more, then lifted the bed sheets aside.

'You've had a rigid dressing up till now,' Mr Dev was saying. 'Like a light plaster cast. If things are good, we'll replace it with soft dressings — a lot of bandages.' He was bent over Ben's vanished leg, hands moving. 'Tell us if it hurts, remember. Don't try to be too brave.'

Ben tried to breathe deeply and slowly, like he'd done with Hom. There was one tug that made him catch his breath and clench his fists for a second, then the feeling of something being lifted from around his knee. *What did it look like down there? How ugly would his . . . his stump be? Was he gonna call it that — a stump?*

'Excellent.' Mr Dev nodded. 'The wound is healing very well. We will wait for another day before you take your photo, then you'll be almost ready to go home.'

Ben knew his mouth was half-open again. 'Go — home?'

The surgeon smiled. 'You like it so much here that you want to stay? We'll try you in a wheelchair till you feel confident, then off you go.'

He was wrapping something below Ben's knee. Something softer, lighter-feeling than whatever had been there before. The big male nurse went out, with a little tray holding a wad of stiff-looking white cloths. There were dark brown blotches on some of them. *Bandages with my blood*, Ben realised. *Gross!*

Mr Dev came back to the head of the bed. 'Going home is only the beginning, Ben. You will need the wheelchair, then crutches, till the wound is absolutely healed. Then the prosthetist will start making your new leg. A custom-built one! You can even choose a special paint job if you want. That will mean many appointments and much practice.' The surgeon stretched his shoulders. *He's tired, too*, Ben realised.

'You are a walker, I hear? A tramper?' Mr Dev asked. Ben nodded. 'With your new leg, you can do that again. Very carefully, and never quite the way it was. As I say, let us be truthful about that. But you can do it if you want. Do you?'

'Yes.' Ben said it again, louder. 'Yes, I do. Thanks, Mr Dev. Thanks heaps.'

I'm going to do it, he told himself when he was alone once more. *I'm going to get back up on Pangonui and walk. I'll see those boulders and the bush again.*

Thirty seconds later, he was flat on his back and fast asleep.

This time it was Hom who woke him, as she arrived pushing a little trolley into the room. 'You are looking much better. Are you ready to try some leg exercises?'

What leg? Ben thought. Then he remembered — his best shot — and went 'Yeah'.

First he did more arm-moving and breath-holding. And the embarrassing bum-clenching. Then Hom folded back the bed sheets from around his waist. (*My undies!* Ben thought again. *I'm not still wearing the same pair, am I?*) From the trolley, she took two small pillows, slid one carefully under his right thigh, and the other *very* carefully under his left thigh. 'Now, you lift your right leg. Just a little way. Good. Hold. Good. Down. We do this ten times.'

By the time he finished, his right leg felt more real, somehow. Real, and a bit stiff. *Every hour I lie here, I'm getting weaker*, he realised. *Yeah, I've gotta get up and get moving.*

Hom slipped her hands under his left thigh. 'Very gentle, you lift your left leg. Just like ordinary, but slow. I will hold it, so you do not drop and hurt. Ready? Up.'

Now it comes, Ben knew. Something he'd done without thinking all his life was changed forever. He tried to raise his left leg, just like he'd raised the other. Nothing happened.

He heard himself gasping. 'Can't! I can't!'

'Do not worry. It is often like that after such a shock. Imagine you are getting up in the morning. You push back the bed sheets like I have done. Now you lift your left leg to start getting out of bed. I hold you, remember. Ready? Up.'

Ben tried again. His heart was starting to thump. Still nothing. His left thigh started to stiffen slightly, but it wouldn't lift up. 'I — I can't!' He knew his voice was shaking.

'Do not worry,' Hom said once more. 'Just the trying is good for muscles. We do two more times.'

Ben sucked in a breath, tried as if he were pushing up against the boulder that had smashed down on him. Nothing. Another time. Still no movement.

'Enough for today,' went Hom. 'We will try tomorrow. Sometimes it takes a longer while. We must not damage Mr Dev's lovely stitches.'

She began to smile at Ben. Then she lowered his useless left thigh, moved up to the head of his bed, and stood holding his hand, while he wept and wept as if he would never stop.

SEVEN

Hom passed him some tissues. Then some more tissues. 'Don't worry. It is often like this. Your body has to learn new ways.

'Now,' she went on. 'You are still having pains? Where the leg was?'

Ben nodded. If he tried to speak, he'd choke up. 'I can help with that,' The physio said. 'We start telling your brain what is real and what is not.' She took a small bottle from her trolley, poured some oily liquid onto one palm, then rubbed her hands together. 'This is olive oil and Vitamin E mixed. Good for damaged skin and tissue. I will massage the residual limb — the remaining part of your leg. Being massaged signals your brain that it is really there. Slowly the brain learns what are real feelings and make-believe feelings. Tell me if it is sore. Do not be too brave.'

The hands moved around his knee, pressing, digging gently into the flesh. Then the back of his leg, where the calf muscle began. *What has Mr Dev done with all the nerves and muscles and stuff there?* Ben wondered. After a few minutes, he went, 'That's g— that's good,' and was pleased to hear his voice sounding steady.

Hom nodded. 'It will not stop all the phantom pains, and the feelings you think you have. Some people keep these feelings for twenty years. But it helps. Now, I pinch your skin for the same reason. Tell me if I am too hard.'

It actually felt quite nice. Little nips all around his knee and further down. Four or five minutes, then Hom replaced the protective cradle, and folded the bed sheets back over it. 'Good. Now you rest. I see you tomorrow.'

Another bedpan — he'd remembered they were called that, but never imagined he'd end up using one. The nurse left it with him, came back five minutes later, took it away with a cloth over it. He didn't feel totally embarrassed this time. Only nearly totally embarrassed.

His parents came again. His mother still looked tired. As she sat down, Ben said, 'Sorry, Mum.' She began to speak, made a hiccupping noise, reached for a handkerchief. Ben's father laughed and put his hand on her shoulder. 'Stop making your mother cry, son. You know how good she is at it!' Mrs Coles half-laughed as well. She took Ben's hand and squeezed it. *Ouch!* he thought. *My brain felt that, all right.*

He told them what Mr Dev had said about going home, and the wheelchair. His dad nodded. 'That's great, eh, buddy? We've got lots of things ready for you. Mr Dev suggested a couple of things to help.'

'Dad and Uncle Kyle have been taking some doors off, love,' his mother added. Ben stared, and she said, 'So you can get the — the wheelchair into places easier.'

They stayed for twenty minutes. Ben didn't say anything about the exercises and how he couldn't move his left leg. Neighbours all along the street had sent their best wishes, his mum told him — Mrs Tully and Mrs Bhatiani and lots of others.

More texts from Connor and Manu, Ben found when he was alone. He replied to both. *Thanx guys. Feeling stuffed.* He was. He slept again, till a trolley pushed by a smiling woman — *Lagi*, said her name badge — brought his dinner. Fish cakes: cool. Broccoli: not so cool. He seemed to be tasting things more; his body was coming back to life. Pity it was a ruined body now.

He slept on and off through the night. Twice, someone came into his room. 'Do you want any pain control, Ben? Do you want me to move you?' a voice asked. He mumbled 'No', shifted himself sleepily. *Ouch!* went his left foot, and his eyes flicked open, till he remembered.

He lay for what seemed like an hour, staring at the ceiling, hearing noises from the corridor. A few cars passed on the road outside. His parents had talked about giving him some driving lessons; about how Ben might start planning for his Learner Licence next year, maybe. But would he ever be able to drive a car now? Or even ride his bike again? There must be ways, but —

And how would he be able to handle school? Even sit at a desk? He couldn't do PE, or hang out with his mates at lunchtime. And . . . what would he look like to girls? There were some really cute ones in his classes.

Suddenly he felt wild at himself. He was still a person. He was still *himself*. Why should his changed look matter to a girl?

His back hurt. His left leg didn't, for a change. After a while, he half-slept once more.

Sausages and hash browns for breakfast. 'Make sure you eat your fruit and cereal, too,' said the woman who brought it. Her name badge read *Shu Min*. 'I know what teen boys are like.'

The dishes had just been cleared away when Hom arrived with her trolley. 'You are looking wide awake. Ready for your next gym session?'

'What if —' Ben's throat felt tight. 'What if I still can't lift my leg?'

His physio was moving aside the bed sheets. 'Do not worry, remember? I told you that it takes time. First we warm up. Do not rush.'

He stretched arms, back, neck, tightened his bum. *Maybe I* will *tell Manu and Connor about this*, he decided. *But if they tell anybody else, I'll bloody murder them.*

With Hom's help, he lay flat and lifted his right leg, eight . . . ten times. His heart was starting to thump again. In a minute, he'd find out.

'You are not to worry, remember,' Hom said, as she moved her hands underneath his left thigh. 'Now try to raise — Yes!'

His left leg — the remains of his left leg — was already off the sheet, lifting up. He panted a couple of times, raised it higher. 'Enough!' Hom told him. 'You must not strain Mr Dev's lovely stitching, remember.

Hold up. Now slowly down. Very good! Just five more this side.'

It worked perfectly. He pictured himself getting out of bed, like she'd told him to imagine yesterday. He sent the message to his brain; moved his left thigh and knee. Up went the left leg again, so fast this time that it left Hom's supporting hands behind. 'You are not doing the high jump!' she laughed. 'Not so quick!'

'Two — more!' grunted Ben, when he had finished the first six. Hom began to shake her head, then said, 'All right. But slowly.'

He raised his left leg again. Once. Twice. He held it in the air, a bandage-wrapped shape he could just see from where he lay on his back, till his physio told him 'Enough. Down — slowly.'

She smiled at him, where he lay puffing. 'You are a superman, I think.' Then she reached for her box of tissues, as Ben began weeping again.

EIGHT

'Sorry,' he gasped, after a while. 'I was scared I couldn't do it. Not ever.'

Hom passed him a fourth — or maybe fifth — tissue. 'I sometimes see big men cry. Many who work in forests, or boats. I use lots of tissues.' She reached for her trolley. 'I will give your residual leg a massage.'

'It's not hurting much,' Ben told her, but she shook her head. 'Your brain needs training, remember. Ha! *All* boys' brains need training!'

The pressure all around his knee and below. The pinching. 'What happened to my muscles?' Ben heard himself ask. 'The ones in my leg, I mean. They're still working, so what did Mr Dev do?'

His physio nodded. 'When there is an amputation,

surgeons cut the bones right back, so they do not push through the stump. They make the ends round; then they do not hurt the tissue. They sew muscles to other muscles. Or to bones. They leave as much skin as they can . . .' She glanced at Ben as she began replacing things on her trolley. 'You do not mind knowing this? Sometimes, the big men start to faint when they hear.'

Ben shook his head. 'It's OK.' Actually, it was quite interesting, in a weird sort of way.

'The skin makes a fold over the wound,' Hom went on. 'Mr Dev is brilliant. Perhaps he learns to sew at school?' She smiled down at Ben. 'Very well done. I will see you this afternoon.'

As he lay there, Ben tried again. He felt muscles tighten all along his body: back, bum, thighs, knee. His left leg rose till it almost nudged the cradle beneath his bed sheets. He held it; lowered it; repeated the movement twice more. Jeez, a human body was amazing. He'd never really thought about it till now. Till it was too late.

Mr Dev arrived just before lunch, with the same big, shaven-headed male nurse. There was more heart-listening, blood-pressure measuring and temperature-taking. Then the surgeon said, 'I'm going to change your dressings again, Ben. Do you feel like taking a look at things? Only if you want to.'

Ben hesitated, then nodded. 'Yeah.' The big nurse lifted him gently; propped pillows behind his back. 'Shout out if you get dizzy, buddy. You've spent a long time lying down.'

Mr Dev had already turned back the bed sheets and removed the cradle. It was made of white plastic. Ben stared down, and his first thought was that something had gone missing. Then he saw. His left thigh was scratched and bruised-looking. Below his knee, the leg continued to where his calf and shin should be. Then came a wad of white bandages. And then . . . nothing. Empty space. Beside it stretched his right leg, also scratched, but whole and perfectly normal. He gazed, swallowed, tried to make sense of it.

'Don't worry if you feel frightened,' Mr Dev was saying to him. 'It's a big shock. Your brain has been told, but it still can't quite believe.'

Ben said nothing. He couldn't. The surgeon began to unwind the bandages, and Ben's missing foot gave a stab which made him gasp. 'Pain?' Mr Dev asked instantly. 'We can give you —'

Ben shook his head. 'It was my foot. The one that's . . . not there.'

The surgeon nodded as he kept unwrapping. 'Someone has hacked your computer. Think of it like that. Your brain and nerves are sending you scrambled messages. Your body will learn to unscramble them, but it takes time.'

Ben could see some of the skin below his knee now. It looked the same as usual, just a bit pale, with marks where the dressings had been. Mr Dev glanced up at him. 'You will notice some signs of blood, but the arteries and veins have healed very well indeed. The stitches look big and black, but that is normal.'

Three, four turns, and the final bandage came off. Mr Dev placed it in a basin that the shaven-headed nurse held, and bent over the leg, murmuring 'Excellent. Clean and healthy. Very good indeed.'

Ben meanwhile sat, staring and staring at the cut-off remains of what had once been a growing thing. Halfway between knee and where his left ankle had once been, the skin and flesh seemed to swell out suddenly. Below that, they were folded over, tucked up like the end of a parcel. He could partly see the stitches. Nine . . . ten rows of them, running across, from front to back.

And everything else was gone. He'd been told, but

now he could actually see it. The bones and muscles and flesh on which he had walked and run and kicked a rugby ball had vanished forever. He kept staring. He didn't feel sick or scared, just numb. And sad, somehow.

Mr Dev was still talking. 'No dog ears; very good.' He saw Ben's expression and smiled. 'Sometimes the stitches leave awkward little flaps of skin that we have to cut off later. Dog ears, we call them. But yours are fine. I will put another dressing on, to protect it for the next few days.'

'It looks . . . thicker.' At Ben's words, the surgeon nodded once more. 'Fluid from the body's defences builds up near the wound. We call it oedema. It's a normal part of healing, can come and go for a few weeks, sometimes longer. That's why we don't try to fit your prosthesis — your new leg — till it's settled down properly.'

The big nurse had left the room. Now he returned again. Ben's eyes widened as he saw the nurse was pushing a wheelchair.

'Jake here —' Mr Dev nodded at the nurse, who gave Ben a grin, '— will help you start getting out of bed. If everything goes well, you'll be home in two, maybe three days.'

He held up a hand as Ben opened his mouth. 'You must use the chair for a week or so till the wound has completely healed. Then crutches till the oedema has settled. Your physio . . . Hom, I think it is?' (Jake nodded; seemed to grin slightly.) '— She will come to you. Lots of exercise, too, Ben, and the physio treatment will keep going even after you get your prosthesis. You understand all that?'

'Dad says — he says we're going to go tramping again.'

The surgeon smiled once more. 'As I told you before — why not? We have people who run races with prostheses, or who climb mountains. But you must be patient, Ben. It will take time. And you must be careful at first. Your body is unbalanced now; you weigh less on one side than the other. On the crutches, you will feel this.' He paused a moment. 'I will see you again, but now I leave you to Jake.'

Mr Dev left. The big nurse lifted something from the seat of the wheelchair. A square of wood like a tray, with four little wheels under it.

'Here we go, buddy. Don't expect you to make it onto the chair today, but we'll start practising. It's . . . what? Well over a week now since you did any real moving around, so you'll be weaker than you think. And like the doc says, you've got to learn balancing yourself again. So we'll start with just getting you to sit on the edge of the bed, OK?'

'OK.' Ben began turning himself sideways, stopped and grunted as his hips and back both complained at once.

'Take it easy. No hurry, remember.' Jake held up the wheeled tray in one big hand. 'I'm gonna put this under your backside. It'll help you move around till you've got the knack of things again. Now just relax.'

Ben felt one hand under the small of his back, gently raising him. The other hand was around his shoulders. 'I've got you, mate. Just say if it hurts. And mind Mr Dev's sewing, or he'll stitch *me* up. Here we go.'

Ben half-swivelled his body, pushed himself away from the pillows. He felt the little tray roll forward beneath his bum. Jake held him, murmured 'Slowly . . . good . . . ease forward . . . bit more. You're there!'

He was sitting on the edge of the bed, right foot almost touching the floor, left leg bent, with the stump pointing down. Below the knee, his own flesh and skin, then the white bandages, and then that nothingness. He heard himself panting.

'Just sit there for a moment,' Jake told him. 'Like I say, you're likely gonna feel dizzy.'

He was. The walls seemed to shift sideways around him, and specks flickered in front of his eyes. His neck ached. 'Breathe slow,' Jake told him. 'Slow and deep.

You've been practising that with Hom?'

Ben dragged in air, let it out, did so again. The giddiness faded.

'Better?' Jake asked. When Ben nodded, the nurse said, 'OK. Now you count to ten. Then you lie back and do it all three times more.'

He did. By the third time, he was able to do most of the sideways moving by himself. Mr Dev was right; the left side of his body felt lighter than the other. When he sat up, he kept tilting towards the right; would have toppled once if Jake's arm hadn't steadied him. But he was able to stay upright on the bed edge, even shuffle along it on his bum.

'Good stuff,' grinned the big nurse. 'OK, buddy, you've earned a rest.'

Ben shook his head. 'Wheelchair. I want to —'

Jake looked uncertain. 'You reckon? Don't rush it, remember.'

'No, I want to. Please?'

The nurse reached out, pulled the chair close beside the bed. 'All right. We talk how first, then we try it. Just once.'

And Ben began coming back into the world again.

NINE

Three days later, he went home. His father wheeled him along the hospital corridor, while figures in green or blue or maroon uniforms bustled by. A fair-haired girl his age, wearing a red mitten on one hand, passed them, heading the other way. She looked at Ben, so he looked hard back at her. *What you staring at?* he felt like saying.

He'd got out of bed and into the wheelchair six or eight times each day, till he could do it by himself, provided he sat on the edge of his bed for a few seconds first. He had to be helped from chair back into bed because the wheelchair was lower. 'It's just a basic one, buddy,' said Jake, as he eased Ben onto the sheet, and Ben hauled himself across. 'No flashing lights or missile launchers, sorry. Hopefully you won't be in it for long.'

He'd been to the loo. Jake had to half-lift him onto the seat, which was embarrassing. It'd be even more embarrassing with a female nurse, but anything was better than those bedpans.

'Hold on to these.' Jake pointed at metal rails bolted to the wall beside the loo. 'You're still a bit lopsided, remember. Don't want you falling off, halfway through.'

He'd done more stretching and moving (and bottom-clenching) and leg-lifting with Hom. 'I come to your house Tuesdays and Thursdays.' (Oh man, would he have to tidy his room?) He'd been checked again by Mr Dev. 'I'll see you if there are any problems, don't worry. We're a busy place, but you'll get gold star treatment till you're fully recovered.'

The surgeon paused. 'Your parents will be keeping an eye on your dressings; we've talked about that. We need to make sure the wound stays clean till it's one hundred per cent healed. One hundred and ten per cent, in fact. Mustn't allow any infection.'

The little tray with wheels was already in his mum and dad's car, along with a bag of bandages, painkiller pills, a jar of olive oil and Vitamin E for massaging his stump. 'Use it twice a day,' Hom told him. 'You do it. Or your parents, if you feel lazy.'

She'd also reminded him to keep doing his exercises,

especially the new ones she'd taught him in the last three days. Long quads, where he lay on his back and stretched his legs. Short quads, sitting propped up against pillows and lifting one leg, then the other. He could raise his left leg every time now. His neck and back ached a bit less. His left ankle and foot still stabbed sometimes.

Once, as he sat gazing at the half-limb with its bandages (*What* was *he going to call it? Stump? Residual leg? Oh well, he'd have plenty of time to decide*), he felt an itch in the big toe, so real that he began leaning forward to scratch it. He stopped, pinched and massaged his leg above the amputation, like Hom had shown him, and the itch slowly faded. It was all so weird.

Yes, his mother had told him; they'd talked to Mr Dev — and to Hom — about what to do when he was home. They had pages of instructions and advice for every day: how to protect the stump in bed by wedging cushions or pillows alongside it; checking how it felt every day ('Too hot means it could be getting infected,' his mum recited. 'Too cold means blood circulation might not be working properly. It has to be just right — like Goldilocks' porridge.') She smiled at him; touched his cheek. She'd been doing a lot of that while he was in hospital.

The main doors slid open, and they were outside. Ben had to half-close his eyes. The lights inside had been bright, but out here, the sun flooded everything. And the air smelled different: cool, fresh, the scent of flowers and trees and — yeah, petrol fumes.

His father wheeled him towards the car, easing the chair over every little rut and bump. 'It's OK, Dad,' Ben told him. 'Doesn't hurt. Pedal to the metal, eh?' It was the first joke he'd made since his life had changed, and straightaway he felt better.

They reached the parking spot, and Ben blinked as he saw the yellow mobility symbol, a wheelchair, painted on the ground in front. Hell, he'd always thought those parking spaces were just for old people. He'd never imagined . . .

Mr Coles opened the front passenger door, and Ben saw that its seat had been pushed back as far as possible, with the wheeled tray placed on it. 'That big nurse guy came and showed me.' His father looked down at Ben. 'Out of the chair and onto this tray first.'

'Getting into a car's just like getting onto the loo,' Jake had told them. 'Except it's a two-hundred horse-power loo.' As his dad began to reach forward, Ben went, 'Wait. Park the chair parallel to the seat, then I'll lower the armrests.'

His dad eased the wheelchair into place. Ben unclipped and lowered its arms. He said 'Wait' again; gazed into the car. Its seat was almost the same height as the chair. Left-hand side of the car, so his residual limb (he'd got used to the hospital language now) would come in last.

He reached his right leg inside, leaned forward and gripped the dashboard. 'OK. Hold me under the arms. When I say, lift and move me forward.' It felt weird to be giving his father orders. 'Ready. Now.'

His dad lifted. Ben pulled on the dashboard. He half-slid, half-flopped onto the little tray. As he landed, he remembered his lopsided weight. Too late: his body lurched to the right, his left leg swung inside after him, and thumped against the seat. 'Aah!' he yelled. 'Aah!'

Straightaway, his father was crouching beside him, eyes frightened. The wheelchair lay toppled on its side, one wheel spinning. A couple of people nearby turned to stare.

'Oh, son!' his dad panted. 'Mate, you all right?'

Ben sat, staring at his leg inside its pinned-up jeans, waiting to see blood turning his bandages sodden and scarlet. Mr Dev's stitches would be torn open. He'd have to go straight back into the theatre, while they . . .

But the bandages didn't change colour. There was no pain from the stump. He'd bumped the side of his leg, not the wound itself. He was frightened, but not really hurt.

He tried to breathe deeply. 'I'm OK,' he told his father, who still crouched, gripping his shoulders. When his dad kept holding him, he went, 'I'm *OK*!' More people turned to stare.

Very quietly, Mr Coles closed the passenger door. As he got in the driver's side, Ben was pulling his seat-belt into position. His father pointed to the wheeled tray underneath his son. 'You want that moved?' Ben shook his head.

They drove out of the hospital grounds and headed towards home. Ben knew that his dad was being three times more careful than usual. He sat, half-squinting at the dazzling leaves on trees and hedges as they passed, breathing deep the way Hom had taught him.

'Didn't mean to yell at you,' he said, after a couple of streets. 'Got a fright.'

'Makes two of us.' Mr Coles reached across, and gently punched his son on the shoulder. Ben nodded at the road ahead. 'Drive carefully, eh? I might not be able to jump out the window if we crash.' They both snorted.

'Whole lot of stuff for you at home,' his father said, a few more streets further on. 'Cards and books and stuff from people. Manu came round, left a massive box of chocolates from your form class. Your mum and I can help with those, if you like.'

Ben snorted again. He already knew that none of his friends were allowed to visit him for another week at least, same as they couldn't come to see him in hospital. The drugs he'd had before and just after his operation could weaken his immune system for a while, Mr Dev had told him. He mustn't take any risk of catching a virus — of catching *anything* — till he was fully healed. So thank God for texts.

'Oh, and Mrs Sione came round, too. Said you were excused your English assignment, but don't think this is going to get you off homework for the rest of the year.'

I'll do that homework, Ben told himself. *After all, I've got to keep beating my best mate in English — and in Social Studies.*

They reached their street. Mr Coles turned carefully into it, drove slowly along, began easing the car into the driveway. 'Here's your mum. She wanted to have the house all open when you arrived.'

But Ben wasn't looking at his mother, as she came smiling towards the car. He was gazing past her, towards the side door they always used. On top of the concrete steps leading up to it lay something new. A wooden deck, angling down to the driveway. A wheelchair ramp.

That was his life from now on. Ten . . . eleven days ago, he'd walked down those steps to go tramping, like a normal person. Now he'd never be normal again.

TEN

His mother leaned in; kissed him on the cheek. 'Welcome home, darling.' His dad helped him from the car and into the wheelchair. 'Make sure — the brake's on,' grunted Ben, as he swivelled on the little tray, and began moving his half-leg out of the door. His father started to say 'Can we —', but Mrs Coles lifted a hand, and he stopped.

The weight of his right leg would drag him back this time, he knew. 'Turn the chair to face the front of the car and keep its arms down,' he went. 'Then hold it.' His father gripped the wheelchair. Ben stretched forward, seized its near handle with both hands, then heaved himself off the car seat and into the chair, half-turning as he did so.

There was one scary moment when he knew he wouldn't make it; would crash onto the path and tear his stitches apart. His mother gasped; his dad started to jerk forward. Then he was in the wheelchair, breathing deep.

'You're a real pro!' his mum exclaimed, and Ben realised she'd been more frightened than he was. His father patted him on the shoulder. 'No problems, eh, buddy?'

His dad pushed him up the ramp to the side door. As the chair tilted backwards, Ben gripped its arms.

The hallway looked different, somehow. Brighter and emptier. Then he saw that the little table on which his mum always kept a vase of flowers had vanished. And — yeah — light was flooding in from his bedroom, and from the bathroom further on, where the doors had been taken away. He remembered his mother saying how Uncle Kyle and his father had been doing that; now he saw what she'd meant. *There's gonna be problems for others, too*, he realised. *Who's paying for all this? Hey . . . They don't expect me to use the bathroom without a door, do they? Aw, man!*

'Doors are out in the garage.' Ben's dad must have guessed what he was thinking. 'We'll put them back once you aren't using the chair.'

He wheeled his son gently into the dining room. The table was already set for lunch. 'People have been bringing us cakes and scones and all sorts of things,' Mrs Coles told him. 'You hungry?'

'Yeah.' Well, he wasn't, not all that much. But he was hungry for something different from hospital food.

His father began to move his wheelchair towards the table, but Ben said, 'I want to do it.' He gripped the wheels and pushed himself forward, pausing till he was sure his leg-and-a-half could fit under the table. He lowered the chair's arms, held the edge of the table, and pulled himself closer. So he could do this, too. Big deal.

'Good, mate.' His father stood watching. 'Now, I know there's all these cakes and stuff, but I was talking to one of the nurses at the hospital and she told me what you want most for your first meal at home. You ready?'

Ben stared. 'What —'

His mother came through from the kitchen. In her hands, she held a plate. On the plate was a colossal burger.

'You want a rest now, darling?' Mrs Coles asked, after Ben had eaten the burger, some cakes and biscuits, and a couple of chocolates from the box Manu had brought.

'I better do some exercises after that.' Ben nodded at

the empty plates. He felt . . . stronger after the meal. Stronger, and too full.

'I've made some space in the living room, mate,' his father said. 'Or do you want to lie on your bed and do them?'

Ben's mum was starting to clear the table. That had always been one of his jobs after meals. Now he heard his mouth go, 'I'll do those.'

'It's all ri—' his mother began, but he spoke louder. 'I'll do it, OK?'

His parents sat in their places and said nothing. Ben wheeled himself slowly around the table, grunted as his wheelchair bumped it. His dad reached out a hand, but he shook his head. 'It's all right. Let me.' He took plates, manoeuvred himself to the bench and stacked them. After the first attempt, when he held a plate in one hand, tried to push his chair with the other, and turned in a small circle instead, he started to get the hang of it.

It took him only about eight times as long as it had before . . . before what happened on the mountain. Another big deal.

Yeah, there was space in the living room, but he wheeled himself into his bedroom. The chair where he usually chucked stuff had gone, and his desk had been moved along. There was a TV on a wall bracket, facing his bed. *Cool!* The room looked bigger and barer.

He held the side of his bed and lowered the wheelchair's arms. Could he pull himself up onto the bed? If he put his right leg on the ground, he could sort of twist himself out of the chair and up. He was moving his good leg into position when his father knocked at the doorway and came in. 'Wait,' his dad went.

Ben didn't look at him. 'I can do it,' he said again. He reached for the bed's side once more.

'Wait!' Mr Coles spoke loudly. 'Look, son, I know you want to try things for yourself. But just now, the most important thing is to let that leg heal.' He paused for a moment. Ben said nothing. 'If you damage it, things get so much harder for you. And for the rest of us, eh? That includes your mum. So let me help for a bit. Tell me what to do.'

With his dad keeping one arm around him and protecting the leg with his other hand, Ben got himself up and onto the bed. He lay there, letting out his breath.

His father watched him. 'Can I stay with you while you do the exercises?' Ben started to speak, but his dad kept talking. 'I know you can manage, but I want to learn, too, OK?'

Ben was silent. After a few moments, he started the deep breathing, the arm-lifting and bum-clenching that he now knew off by heart. *I'm a bit stronger*, he realised.

'Your physio,' Ben's father said, when his son had finished lifting each leg twelve times. 'She says that next week, you can start adding some weights to your legs. She seems really good.'

Ben grunted. He began reaching behind him for a pillow, to tuck under his thighs during the long quad and short quad exercises. He half-toppled, stuck a hand down to stop himself, began reaching behind again. His dad moved forward. 'Let me. No, mate — you're twisting and straining to reach it. Don't *rush*!'

Father and son locked eyes for a moment. Then Ben rolled on his right side while Mr Coles pushed a pillow beneath him. 'There? Good.'

The man stood back and watched silently. When Ben had finished his quad stretches, he lay for a moment, then muttered, 'I need to sit up.'

Without saying anything, his dad took him under the arms, lifted while Ben pushed, till he was propped up. He stood by the bed while Ben did the trunk rotations, shoulder-liftings and neck-turnings that Hom had started him on, a few days before he left hospital.

'Quite a workout, mate,' The man said, when Ben finally stopped. His son nodded. 'Helps.'

'You want a coffee or a Coke or something?' his father asked. He nodded at the head of the bed. 'TV remote's there on a cord, if you need it.'

Ben shook his head. 'Nah. Think I'll just blob for a bit.' His dad pointed to the bedhead again. 'There's a call button there, too. Hospital loaned it to us. Just press it if you need anything.'

Ben closed his eyes and didn't reply. He heard his father leave the room. A hospital call button. A help for the helpless. The useless.

Then — *No!* he thought. *I'm not gonna be useless. Hom said so. I'm gonna get that new leg — soon, I hope. I'm gonna get back to being me.*

ELEVEN

When Ben woke, the sunlight had moved across his bedroom floor. 3.35 p.m. Manu and Connor and his other mates would be starting to walk home from school. Walking and shoulder-punching and joking like they always did.

He had a problem. He lay for a few minutes, reached for the call button, stopped and raised his voice instead. 'Mum? Dad?'

It was his mother who came into the room, smiling at him. Yeah, she looked tired. 'Hello, love. Had a rest?'

'I need to go to the loo.'

'Oh, all right. The hospital gave us —'

'I'm not using a bedpan. I'm not!'

'That's not what I was going to say, Ben. They've given

us a raised seat for the toilet, so you can get onto it easier.'

Mr Coles appeared in the doorway. He watched as Ben swivelled himself around till he was sitting on the edge of the bed. Ben's mother began to move forward, then stopped herself.

'Can you put the wheelchair right beside me?' Ben asked.

His father was gazing at where he sat. 'How about I get your Uncle Kyle to bolt a couple of handgrips to the sides of your bed? That should make it easier to get on and off.'

Ben looked, nodded. 'OK.' As he started to speak again, Mr Coles said, 'Let us help the first couple of times, eh? Just till you're more used to things.'

Ben shrugged. But as his father helped ease him from the bed into the chair, and his mother wheeled him to the bathroom ('Oouff! You're heavier than when I did this with your pushchair!'), he knew his parents were right. There were so many things — basic, little kids' Things — that he couldn't do for himself.

It took his mother five tries to position wheelchair beside toilet. Ben was staring at its new, high seat, and a metal handrail bolted to the wall on the far side. 'Your dad and Uncle Kyle did that, too. The hospital suggested it in one of the pamphlets they gave us.'

Does that mean Mum and Dad are having to pay for all this stuff? Ben wondered again. He remembered the handrails beside the hospital's loos and lowered the arms of his chair. 'Mum, could you —'

To his surprise, his mother laughed. 'I wiped your bottom enough when you were little. I won't try now.' She pointed at the doorless doorway, where a curtain now hung. 'I'll pull that across so you're private. You can do it for yourself next time. Do call out if you need us, darling.'

When she was gone, Ben sat for a moment; gazed at the new toilet seat. Same height as the chair: yeah, that would help. He put the wheelchair's brake on, reached across to grip the rail with his right hand, and heaved himself up.

Again, there was a second of fear when he was in midair and could have toppled anywhere. But the movement was a fraction easier and more confident this time. *I can sit on the loo by myself,* he thought. How pathetic.

He replied to some more texts. *Sumthing gr8 4 U 2nite*, Manu's read. What? He ate dinner with his parents and cleared the table again. It took him only *seven* times as long as normal. His missing leg gave little . . . flickers now and then, like an insect was walking on it. But there was hardly any pain.

When he'd finished doing the table, his dad grinned at him. 'Something you might like to have, buddy. Connor and Manu brought it round this morning. Want to come through to the living room?'

The hall carpet was thicker at the living room doorway. The wheelchair stuck. Ben pushed it back, then forward again. 'Let *me* do it!' he snapped, as his father reached for the handles. He wrenched at the wheels; the chair jerked forward and slewed sideways. One side of the footrest gouged across the doorway, leaving a raw scratch on the varnish. Ben shoved himself into the living room. Neither he nor his dad said anything.

Instead, Mr Coles handed Ben a game controller. 'You're in charge, mate. It looks like some sort of shooting thing. Enjoy — if that's the right word.'

It was a zombie game. His mother poked her head into the room after a while, exclaimed, 'That's so gross! . . . Ewww — that's so disgusting!' and hurried away. His father went out to the garage. Ben sat playing from his wheelchair, and for five minutes at a time, he almost forgot what had happened to him.

He slept OK, woke once and knew there was something strange with his body, found he was lying on his left side, the vanished foot throbbing and stabbing.

He started to turn himself onto his other side, caught his breath as his stump seemed to snag against the pillows packed around it, and lay, trying to control his breathing. All these things he'd have to learn to do all over again.

When he wheeled himself to the bathroom next morning, he found a plastic chair sitting underneath the shower, and another handrail bolted to the wall of the cubicle. He peeled off his T-shirt, hesitated, then called 'Dad?' As Mr Coles appeared, Ben muttered, 'Can you help me onto that chair? And what do I do about . . .'

He pointed to his undies. 'If you can take them off once you're on the chair, fine,' his father said. 'Otherwise, just leave them on.'

His dad helped him out of the wheelchair and onto the plastic one. Mr Coles began to close the shower curtains, then exclaimed, 'Nearly forgot. Wait.' He left the bathroom, came back with a big, elastic-topped plastic bag. 'Goes over the bandages. Hospital loaned it to us.' He slid the bag over Ben's stump, patted his son on the shoulder, asked, 'OK if I wait in the hall? Sing out if there's an issue.'

Ben mumbled, 'All right.' Then, as his father was closing the shower curtains again, he said, 'Thanks, Dad.' His father grinned, punched him on the shoulder like before, and pulled the curtains around him.

He managed fine. Wriggling from side to side meant he could take off his undies. He let the water sluice over him. When he'd finished, he called, 'Dad, can I have a towel?'

A hand appeared through the curtain. Drying himself wasn't too bad, either, though it was hard to lift his bum to get the towel under. 'You want some fresh undies?' his father called from the hallway, and the same hand appeared through the curtains once more. 'Take it slow —'

'I'm all right,' Ben told him, sharper than he meant to, then found that getting the underpants on was a lot harder than getting them off. He sat breathing hard when he'd finished; called 'OK'.

When he was in his wheelchair again, his father stepped back and gazed at him. 'You're looking good, buddy.' As Ben started to speak, the man said, 'No, I mean it. Your body looks nearly as fit as it did before things happened. You'll have lost strength because you've just been sitting or lying. But you can start working your way back up right now. For our sake as well as your own.' He grinned at his son. 'End of lecture.'

Ben said nothing. But as he pulled on the T-shirt his dad had handed him, he told himself again. He was going to do it. He was going to fight his way back. And yeah, he was going to start right now.

TWELVE

It lasted two minutes. He pushed himself from bathroom into hall, and along towards the dining room, from where the smell of sausages was drifting. Sausages! On a weekday! Yeah, he was going to make things better, starting —

Pain tore through him. Pain so sudden, so savage, that he yelled. 'Aaah! Aaah!' He hunched forward; tried to seize and free himself.

His mother came rushing through from the kitchen. 'What's wrong, love? What's happened?'

'My foot!' Ben knew his face was twisted in agony. His body shuddered and jerked. He tried again to reach down but couldn't make it. 'Aaah! My foot's caught in the wheel!'

His mother dropped onto hands and knees beside the chair. 'Darling, it's OK. It's nowhere near the wheel. Do —'

'The other leg! It's . . .' Ben went silent as he understood. His mother seemed to realise at the same moment. She folded her arms around him.

'Oh, love, it's what the hospital told you. The phantom pains. Your brain is still getting mixed up, sending wrong signals. Shall I ring the hospital — see if they can suggest anything to help?'

Ben sat hunched in his chair, trying to breathe normally. Pain still pulsed through his missing foot. His dad had appeared in the doorway from the garage and stood watching. 'We'll ask about it, buddy. It gets less, they say, but we'll ask about it.'

How can you ask about something that isn't even there? Ben demanded, inside his head. He sat staring at the dining-room floor. He was supposed to be fighting his way back, and he'd failed straightaway.

He ate hardly any breakfast. 'Gonna lie down,' he told his parents. He wheeled himself out of the dining room, scraping against a table leg and not caring. In his room, he managed to get a grip on the mattress and haul himself up onto the bed, his useless stump flopping onto the duvet. He lay there, staring at the ceiling. His parents were talking in low voices from the dining room.

His left foot was still stabbing and throbbing when a car door closed in the drive, and he heard Hom's voice at the door. So it was Tuesday. No, Thursday. What did any day matter now?

His physio knocked and came into the room. She carried a green bag with a white cross on it. 'Hello, Ben. You had a bad experience, I hear.'

'My foot. I thought it was trapped in the wheel. Felt like it was nearly gonna rip off.'

Hom nodded as she started unpacking her bag. 'The brain plays some really strange tricks sometimes. Have you been massaging and pinching your leg like I showed you?'

'I — not since I got home.'

'I will do it right now. If the pain comes again, you straightaway start the massaging. That way the brain remembers. You can help yourself.'

Yeah, OK, Ben thought. *I could have. I should have.*

Hom worked around his left thigh, his knee, the stretch above his stump. Ben could feel the leg becoming . . . calmer was the word that flicked into his mind. Like it somehow understood what was happening. 'Thanks,' he said, as his physio finished.

Her dark eyes smiled. 'Nearly everyone has bad moments like that. It takes time. Do lots of massage and pinching in the first weeks, all right? But gentle — you can do harder later on if you need. Now, your exercises. We start with breathing.'

'I know how to —' But Hom shook her head. 'We do it all properly. Every part helps the next part.'

So: breathing, arm-lifting, bum-tightening. The trunk-swinging that he'd started before leaving hospital. The short and long quads. The leg-raising that had once seemed so impossible. Hom checked his pulse at the start and the end. 'Good. Now I look at the dressings.' She raised the stump, while Ben watched, and looked all around it. He sat gazing at the emptiness where a perfect leg had been. It still didn't look real, somehow. If the air had flickered, and the same leg reappeared suddenly, he'd just think — *There you are. Where you been?*

'Looking good,' The physio told him. 'No sign of blood. Remember to keep very clean.' From her bag, she took a tape measure, and fixed it around his upper calf, just above the bandages. 'Hardly any oedema, either. Mr Dev will be pleased. You are seeing him tomorrow?'

Tomorrow was . . . Friday. 'Yeah,' he replied.

‘He will check your sutures. Your stitches. Perhaps you will start on crutches in a few days.’ Ben shrugged. Hom watched him for a moment; said nothing.

Later, his mother brought him a coffee and some chocolate biscuits. ‘Are you sore, love? The hospital gave us plenty of pain medication, remember?’

Sore? His neck and back and hips ached. His missing foot twinged. There was a stabbing pain where his ankle had been, and his vanished toes kept itching. ‘I’ll be all right,’ he said.

‘And we’ve got that olive oil and Vitamin E cream,’ Mrs Coles went on. ‘How about I give your leg a massage? You can tell me how Hom does it.’

Ben started to shake his head. He stopped as he realised something. Neither of his parents had gone to work, not today, not yesterday. His mum taught economics at the local polytech; his dad had a furniture store. They’d both had to stay away from work to help him. This must all be costing them. He was silent for a second, then he muttered ‘OK’.

His mother’s fingers were surprisingly strong. He felt the muscles of his thigh and the top of his calf grow warm and relax. *I’ll thank her when she’s finished*, he decided, and yawned. Then, at 10.45 in the morning, he was asleep.

THIRTEEN

The rest of Thursday dragged past. He ate lunch: a decent lunch — his appetite had come back after the morning's shock. He carried dishes to the sink. If he turned his wheelchair sideways, he could stack them neatly. His dad had left after breakfast to check on his furniture shop — The Great Indoors. 'Anything you want from town, buddy?'

Yeah, thought Ben. *A new leg.* He shook his head.

'I'd better catch up on a few of those polytech assignments I'm meant to be marking,' his mum said. 'Would you like to lie —?'

Ben shook his head again. 'Been doing that too much. I'll help with the dishes.'

His mum washed. He dried. Putting knives and spoons in the drawer was simple enough, and he was getting pretty quick at turning the wheelchair around, so he could park beside places. He put cups up on their shelf; felt quite pleased with himself.

'Time we got a dishwasher,' he told his mother.

She shrugged. 'There's other things just —' and stopped. Ben thought again of the ramp, all the new handles in the bathroom and bedroom.

'Mum?' he said before he knew he was going to. 'When did you know my leg was . . . was gone?'

Mrs Coles stood gazing out the kitchen window, plate in one hand, brush in her other. 'We knew it was badly broken. Your dad had seen it up on the mountain, and he . . .' She paused for a moment; took a breath. Ben remembered his father's voice gasping 'His leg!' as he drifted in and out of consciousness.

'We were at the hospital while you were in the operating theatre.' His mother's voice wobbled. Ben dried two plates without looking at her; wheeled over to put them in the bottom cupboard. 'We'd been waiting and waiting, and then Mr Dev came out. He looked so tired. And sad, somehow. I knew before he even said anything. He did everything he could, love.'

Ben was leaning over to the right, to slide the two

plates down on top of the others. He stretched down, felt a sudden lurch, and his wheelchair tipped sideways. He grabbed at the cupboard door. The plates slipped from his hand, smashing into pieces on the floor. His chair tipped further, till his right side was jammed against the cupboard, his left leg and bandaged stump sticking stupidly up in the air.

'Ben!' There was another crash, from the sink this time, as his mother dropped whatever she'd been washing, and rushed to his side.

'Hold — the chair. Help pull me — up.' Ben pushed against the cupboards; his mother pressed down on the wheelchair's tilted handle, and slowly he came upright again. 'Lost — lost my balance,' he panted after a couple of seconds. To his surprise, he heard himself give a choked-up laugh. 'I keep forgetting how much my leg weighs. Weighed.'

His mother didn't reply. She was crouched with her arms around him, and Ben knew she was trying not to cry.

'Sorry about the plates,' he muttered after a while.

Now his mum lifted her head and looked at him. 'Stuff the plates,' she replied.

When will I see my mates again? Ben wondered, as he sat on his bed later, doing more exercises. His mother was in her study, marking economics assignments. When — how — would he go back to school? And how would the others in Year 10 treat him — like a freak?

He read a bit, dozed a bit. He felt dumb and dull and depressed. His father came home and talked with him. His mother gave his left thigh and knee another massage. After school time, he sent texts to Manu and Connor; got brief replies. *They're out doing things with other guys*, he knew. *They'll forget me before long.*

Friday. His appointment with Mr Dev was at 8.45 a.m. He gave himself an extra ten minutes to shower, found he needed an extra fifteen minutes, grabbed a piece of toast, and was still crunching on it as his father wheeled him down the wooden ramp — 'Tip the chair back! *Right* back, or I'll slide off!' — to the car.

'You give the orders; I'll obey,' grinned Mr Coles after they reached the hospital's mobility parking spot. Swivelling on the small wheeled tray, with his wheelchair parked parallel and his dad holding it firm, Ben moved from one seat to another with no dramas, though he still sat and panted after each transfer. Hell, he must have become so unfit, in spite of his exercises, in spite of his soccer and tramping.

They trundled along the corridor. Ben gazed at the floor; he didn't want to see people's pitying looks. It wasn't till he glimpsed a red mitten that he jerked his head up and saw the same fair-haired girl watching him as she walked past. He just had time to turn his stare into a *whaddaya-looking-at?* glare before she'd gone, along with her stupid mitten.

Fifteen minutes' wait, then they were called into a small room with a bed and a couple of stools. Another five minutes, and Mr Dev bustled in ('Always late. I apologise'), followed by a nurse pushing a trolley with scissors and packages.

She took Ben's temperature. The surgeon checked his pulse and blood pressure. *Reckon I could just about do that myself now*, Ben decided.

'How does the residual limb feel?' Mr Dev asked.

Ben shrugged. 'Hurts, sometimes.'

'Hurts him *a lot* sometimes.' Ben's dad described the moment when Ben thought his foot was trapped in the wheel. The surgeon nodded. 'One patient like you thought somebody had stuck a red-hot iron against his foot. He jumped out of his wheelchair and hopped right across the room.'

Mr Dev drew up a stool. 'Let's see how things are healing.' He lifted Ben's left leg, so it rested on a second stool. 'Not too uncomfortable?' When Ben shook his head, the surgeon turned to the nurse, who passed over the scissors. *Snip, snip*, and Mr Dev began unwinding the bandages. Ben's father stood, arms folded, watching.

Beneath the bandages, wads of gauze covered the stump. The surgeon took a spray bottle. 'The water helps things come off more easily,' he said again. Ben felt the moisture on his calf.

One gauze wad came away smoothly. A second followed. As Mr Dev eased the third away, a stab shot across the stump, and Ben gasped.

The surgeon nodded. 'A little oedemal fluid sticking to things. Healthy-looking fluid, though.' More water, then Mr Dev went, 'Count aloud to four, Ben. Then just one quick tug.'

Ben gripped the arms of his wheelchair. 'One — two —' The surgeon's hand moved, there was a sharp twitch, and Mr Dev was dropping the sodden wad of gauze into a bowl that the nurse held. She smiled at Ben. 'Typical surgeon's trick. Tells you to count to four, then does it on two.'

Mr Dev was bent over the stump, moving it gently in his hands. 'Excellent. It has healed very well.'

He nodded to Ben, then glanced at Mr Coles. So did Ben, and he saw the tears in his father's eyes. 'It's OK, Dad.'

'He is a strong, healthy young man,' The surgeon said. 'I am very pleased. I will take some of the stitches out now, and the rest next week.'

His next words made Ben stare. 'And then we get you on your feet, and back to school again.'

FOURTEEN

'You mean — walking?' Ben knew how stupid the question must sound. But he could hardly believe what the surgeon had just said.

'With help.' Mr Dev took a tape measure from the trolley; began measuring around Ben's stump like Hom had done.

It looks ordinary as well as weird, Ben thought. He could still imagine the rest of it appearing out of thin air and fitting onto the end. The stitches stretched neatly across its surface. The surgeon murmured a figure to the nurse, who wrote it down on a pad. Then he picked up a pair of curved scissors from the trolley.

'On my feet. Walking?' Ben asked again.

'Hmmm? Yes.' Mr Dev bent over Ben's leg again. *Snip*,

snip once more. Scissors, plus some pieces of black thread went back on the trolley. Ben hadn't felt a thing.

'Actually, not completely on your feet yet. You need to keep the wheelchair for a while, till the wound is fully healed.' The surgeon looked at Ben and his father. 'Also, you will feel tired after trying to walk, and the chair is safer in crowds. But the sooner you are standing, the better it is for your body. So next week, we try you with crutches, or a walking frame.'

Crutches or . . . Ben stared. Somehow, he'd been imagining that an artificial leg would magically be ready for him; that he could start walking around, almost like a normal person. Instead . . . Mr Dev's last words echoed in his mind. 'A walking frame? You mean those things old people have?'

'Not only old people,' The surgeon told him. 'Many patients find the frame easier and steadier than crutches. It —'

'I'm gonna have crutches.'

'Ben —' His father was trying not to grin.

Mr Dev chuckled. 'A lot of young people feel the same. Try the crutches first; see how you feel. We will make you an appointment with the Orthotics and Prosthetics team. They look after things like that. But first, I see you next Monday, to take the other stitches out.'

'Can he have his friends over?' Mr Coles asked.

'If they're well. No colds, no stomach bugs. We don't want any extra health issues while you're coping with this. And Ben — no all-night parties, please.'

'That's good about being able to see other people,' Ben's dad said as they drove home.

'I guess.' Ben's stump felt both light and tight. The thick dressings had gone and Mr Dev had fitted an elastic bandage in their place: 'This will feel like it is squeezing your leg a little. That is what we want. It helps keep your residual limb a good size with as little fluid as possible, and that helps the prosthetic fittings. We call it a stump-shrinker. Nice name, eh?'

So the non-leg felt uncomfortable. And his non-ankle was stabbing, and his non-toes were itching. Plus he kept thinking what he was going to look like at school, in a wheelchair or hobbling along on crutches.

His father wheeled him up the ramp into the house. 'Kyle's been,' Mrs Coles told them. 'He's fitted another handle in the shower.'

'Great,' Ben's dad smiled. 'We're all cheering for you, buddy.'

Ben felt totally stuffed. He just wanted to get to his bed and lie down. He'd hoped somehow to be walking when he returned to school, but how was he even going to handle crutches, when being in the wheelchair for a couple of hours wore him out? How was he gonna handle anything?

He felt better after lunch. He did his exercises. He massaged and pinched his leg; then his mum rubbed Vitamin E and olive oil around the stump.

'I'll change your sheets, love,' she said when she'd finished.

'I'll do it. No — I've got to try things, Mum. You can pass me stuff. I'll be careful.'

It was hard, like almost everything now. Stretching to pull the sheets straight meant he had to be careful with his balance. One time, he reached to tuck a corner in; the wheelchair started to tip up, and his mother jerked forward. He held the bed edge, shifted his weight back again.

When he went to the loo ('Call out if you need a hand,' his mum said. 'You've gotta be joking!' Ben told her. 'It's not all that long since I put you on the potty,' she replied), he saw the new metal handle on the shower wall. Yeah, people were cheering for him, like his dad said. Doing things for him. He'd text his Uncle Kyle and say thanks.

There was a message on his phone from Manu. *In boring math, c u afta skool?*

'Manu's coming round,' he called to his mother.

'I told him you could have visitors. All right?'

'Yeah.' Then he added 'Thanks'.

He'd finished his exercises by the time his friend arrived; made himself do extra body turns, plus more short and long quads. The stump-shrinker still pressed, but he was starting to get used to it.

He heard Manu talking to his mother at the front door. 'In here,' he called. Manu's voice came back. 'I know; I just want some intelligent talk first.' Footsteps along the hall, then his best mate appeared.

Manu gazed at the wheelchair, the handle on the wall, the frame where Ben's bedroom door had been removed. He looked at Ben sitting propped up on the bed, a sheet draped over his legs.

Then he crossed the room, said, 'Hey, bro. Really good to see you,' and held out his hand. Ben felt surprised: he and his friends hardly ever shook hands. He felt pleased as well.

'Connor's got Taekwondo.' Manu looked at Ben again. 'How you feeling, bro? I know, everyone's been asking you that, but you managing OK?'

'Yeah.' Well, it was partly true. 'Foot hurts sometimes. The one they cut off.' It was the first time he'd described it that way. It made things seem more definite, somehow.

'Weird. Actually, my koro said the same thing. He had both legs off. Diabetes. Reckoned he used to wake up in the night and want to scratch his left foot against his right foot, even though they'd gone.'

'Your grandad lost *both* legs, eh?' went Ben. 'Bloody showoff.' He and Manu laughed, and Ben suddenly felt heaps better.

'Everyone in the form class says hey,' Manu told him. 'Everyone at *school*, just about. All the girls, even. You got a spare wheelchair I can use, too, have you?' They laughed again.

'You want to see it?' Ben hadn't planned to say the words, but they arrived from some place. 'Where the leg was?'

'Yeah, cool.' Manu thumped himself on the head. 'Sorry, bro. *Not* cool!'

But it was. Ben pushed back the sheet, eased up the elastic stump-shrinker bandage to expose the almost-healed remains. Once again, he thought how ordinary it looked. Ordinary and still hardly believable.

'That's amazing,' Manu said. 'It looks . . . I dunno . . . tidy, sort of.'

'I'm getting crutches next week,' Ben told him. 'Then they'll fit me with a prosthesis. An artificial leg.'

'The Mechanical Man,' Manu grinned. 'The Bionic Beast. Be great to have you back at school, bro. Someone's got to help me look after Connor. Hey, he reckons he's gonna compose a song for when you come back. Sure you don't want to stay away?'

When his friend had left, Ben lay back against the pillows. *So many people and so much going for me*, he thought again. *I'm gonna make it.*

FIFTEEN

Both Manu and Connor arrived on Saturday. ('Hey,' asked Connor, 'you got any of those chocolates left that our class gave you?') Uncle Kyle and Aunt Josie dropped by, too. ('I can fit a handle on you, too, if you want, buddy,' Ben's uncle grinned, when Ben thanked him again for the things he'd done.) Mrs Bhatiani from next door, and Mrs Tully from the other next door, also appeared. 'It's Party Central!' Ben's mother laughed, as she answered yet another knock on the door.

'You want to go for a burn around the block?' Manu asked, after they'd been there for a while. Ben blinked, then said 'Yeah'. With his mother watching, Ben's mates wheeled him and his chair down the ramp, and towards the street.

Last time I came this way, I could walk, Ben thought as they headed along the footpath, Connor and Manu arguing over who was the best pusher. But the sun shone, the leaves glittered, and round the corner, they met two girls from another Year 10 class, who said, 'Hi, Ben, how are you?', and talked to him till Manu went, 'Hey, Connor and me are here, too!'

'Yeah, but you're just ordinary,' one girl — Sally? Polly? Ben was trying to remember — said. Then she glanced at Ben and looked embarrassed. 'Sorry, didn't mean . . .'

'Doesn't matter,' Ben told her. And it didn't, because his two mates pretended to be insulted; reckoned they were going to head off and leave Ben to get home by himself, and the girls exclaimed they were so awful, and everyone laughed, including him, and things were definitely going to be OK.

But he had a bad night. His missing foot felt hot and throbbing. The stump-shrinker cut into his leg below the knee. When he rolled it back in the morning, the flesh above it was puffy and swollen-looking. The stump itself, when he lifted it, seemed clean and healthy. The last couple of stitches were still in place.

'Why don't we take it off for a while?' his mum asked, when Ben told her about the stump-shrinker hurting. 'I'll give you an extra massage, you can try the bandage for another while, and check with Mr Dev when you see him.'

The massage helped. His mother was getting quite expert. Ben did his exercises; used the shower with no problem, except that his undies got damp as he was pulling them up his legs. He yanked at them, yanked harder, tipped sideways and thumped against the wall, grabbing at the new rail. 'Don't rush,' a voice said. It was his own.

As he was getting into bed that Sunday night, he paused before pulling himself out of his wheelchair. He held the edge of his bed with both hands, dragged himself up till he was standing on his right foot. Then he took a breath, let go of the bed, and was upright, wobbling on one leg.

Just for a second, then he lurched sideways and hit his wheelchair, which went skittering across the carpet into the wall. Ben snatched at the bed and crumpled down onto the floor, leg buckling beneath him.

Pain shot through his knee. Pain and terror. What had he done? Then he saw it was his right leg, while the ruined left one sprawled beside it, undamaged. He stared at them both, panting and shuddering.

'Ben?' His father was in the hall. 'You OK?'

'I — yeah.' He made himself speak louder. 'I'm all right. Just pushed the wheelchair away too hard.' He pulled himself slowly up onto the bed. How much longer before he was anywhere near all right? His life seemed to be up and down every day.

Monday morning. His father drove him to the hospital again.

'Reckon they should put our name on this parking spot,' Mr Coles said as they arrived.

'You have any troubles with all this time off work?' Ben felt surprised at his words, but his dad just grinned. 'I'm the owner, remember? The Big Boss. Anyway, sometimes it's good to be outdoors instead of at The Great Indoors.'

The big, shaven-headed nurse Jake ('Hey, buddy; you're looking good') took his pulse, temperature, blood pressure ('they're looking good, too'). Mr Dev came in, greeted father and son. 'Well, Ben, how is everything feeling?'

Ben told him about the uncomfortable stump-shrinker, and the surgeon nodded as he began folding it back. 'Can you put up with it for a couple more days? After you see the prosthetist, he can decide whether to keep it on.'

'When do I see him?'

'You have an appointment at Orthotics on . . . Wednesday, I think? The prosthetist will see you then.'

Jake the nurse grinned again, for some reason. *First, things seem to be taking for ever*, Ben was thinking, *then they all start happening at once.*

Mr Dev took the same curved scissors from the tray Jake held, and once again there came the *snip, snip* from down at Ben's stump. Scissors and a couple of lengths of black thread went back on the tray.

'I am delighted with how things have healed.' The surgeon smiled at Ben, looked at Mr Coles. 'The tissues around the wound will need a little more time to firm up and strengthen, so you must be careful still.'

'When do I get the leg — the artificial one?' Ben hadn't meant to say it so . . . so definitely, but Mr Dev didn't seem worried. 'It will take a number of appointments. The prosthesis must fit as closely and comfortably as possible. You will need the crutches for some time. You may wish to use them even after the leg is fitted.'

I won't, Ben told himself. Mr Dev looked at father and son again. 'I now pass you over to your physiotherapist, plus the Prosthetics team. I hope I do not see you again.' He chuckled. 'I am not being rude. You come to me only if there are complications or infection.' He shook Ben's hand, then his dad's. 'I wish you all the best. It is a long path to full recovery, but you are already on the way.'

As Ben's father wheeled him back down the long corridor (*Yeah, definitely needs a paint job; I guess even hospitals are short of money sometimes*) towards the parking area, Ben tried to decide how he felt. Hopeful, yes. And . . . and important, somehow.

He did his exercises. After lunch, he did more. The fitter he was, the sooner he'd be back to living an ordinary life.

He did some schoolwork as well. Mrs Sione had given Manu a couple of poems for Ben to look at and write a paragraph about. He ate well; slept fairly well.

Hom the physio came to his place on Tuesday. 'So, now I am in charge of you. Be very afraid — is that how you say in New Zealand?' She laughed. *Yeah, she's definitely cute*, Ben decided, *even though she must be nearly . . . oh, twenty-five or something.*

'How is the stump-shrinker feeling?' she asked, as she eased down the elastic bandage.

'Doesn't seem as tight as before.' In fact, he'd hardly thought of it since yesterday. The physio nodded. 'Good. It is doing its job.'

She lifted a bag onto the bed beside him. 'Now I become cruel.' She took out two saggy smaller bags, with long cords. 'These have weights in them. We need to build your strength again for walking. So . . .' She wrapped a cloth around Ben's left leg above the stump, looped the cord of one bag over it, and drew the cord tight. 'Now you practise lifting while I count. Slow and gentle, please.'

One . . . two . . . twelve times, Ben lifted his residual limb. (He still found that name so strange, sometimes; couldn't quite believe it applied to him.) The first four times were easy; the next four harder. By the time he got to ten, his thigh muscles and knee joint were complaining.

He did the same with his right leg. Strangely enough, it didn't feel any stronger than his left one. 'Now we try lifting both legs together with the weights on,' Hom told him. 'Slowly, and I hold your shoulders so you do not fall over.'

This was hard, but good. The first couple of times Ben tried it, his missing left leg meant he began toppling sideways, towards the right. So he leaned his body to that side, which made it easier. By the time he'd done twelve lifts, he was raising both legs and the weights with hardly any balance problems, though his thigh muscles had stopped complaining and started swearing. 'Cool!' he gasped, when he finished.

Hom smiled. 'Well done. You do this twice each day, OK? Your mother or father can help?' Ben nodded. *They'll be pleased to*, he knew.

A massage, another check of the stump, the refitting of the elastic stump-shrinker, and Hom was finished. 'I see you on Thursday. You might have the crutches!'

Next morning, Ben's father parked in the usual hospital spot, then wheeled his son along the usual corridor, turned into a side one, and paused at signs reading *ORTHOTICS; PROSTHETIC WORKSHOP.* Ten metres further on was a waiting room, where half a dozen people sat. A couple of them were in wheelchairs like Ben; a couple more on seats with crutches or walking sticks beside them. A nurse in a dark red tunic stood in front of one chair. An old guy, sitting with one leg tucked under him, moved a newspaper so there was room for Ben's dad and said 'Good morning' in an Irish-sounding accent.

Ben parked his wheelchair beside his father, felt pleased he'd done it neatly, without bumping into anything. The nurse across the room moved away. His dad was saying something to the old guy. No, to him.

'Do you know who you're seeing? Did Hom or Mr Dev give you a name? Ben, you listening?'

He wasn't. Instead, he sat staring across the room, at the chair in front of which the nurse had been standing. And at the person sitting there. A girl with short fair hair. She wasn't wearing the stupid red mitten, though. She was holding it in one hand. The other arm rested on her lap. It ended in a stump.

SIXTEEN

She hadn't seen him. He quickly glanced away, turned to his father. 'Sorry. What?'

'Do you know who you're seeing?'

'No. No, I don't.' The girl had put down the mitten and was on her phone. She still hadn't looked in his direction.

'It'll be either Tessa Mikaere or Tim Wolfe.' Son and father turned as the old guy spoke. 'They're both bonny folk.' *Not an Irish accent*, Ben decided: *a Scottish one*.

'Thanks,' Mr Coles said. 'You've been coming here a while?'

The old guy chuckled. 'Too long. I'm on my third leg.' Ben looked down. The one leg he could see seemed normal. He couldn't tell about the tucked-under one.

A tall woman, also in a dark red tunic, came into the room, and headed in their direction. 'Mōrena, Angus. Like to come along?'

'Your wish is my command, Tessa lass. Can you pass my crutches, laddie?'

Ben saw the metal shapes down by his chair. He bent and picked them up; realised he'd balanced himself without really thinking about it. The crutches felt lighter than he expected. 'Here y'are.'

'Thank you.' The old bloke — Angus — fitted a crutch under each elbow, leaned forward, and heaved himself up, swaying for a second. Ben jerked. The guy hadn't been sitting with one leg tucked under him. From the right knee downward, there was no leg at all.

Too much was happening at once! Ben stared as Angus hopped across the room, both crutches swinging ahead at once, body moving through to take his weight on the left leg, then crutches swinging forward once more. *That's how I'll be doing it*, Ben decided.

He realised he was still staring after the old man, moved his head away, and the girl was watching him.

She still held her phone. The other arm — it ended at

her wrist, and the stump looked like a much slimmer version of Ben's — rested across her lap like before. She was watching him across the room, no expression on her face. But she recognised him; somehow Ben could tell that. She knew him from the times they'd passed in the corridor. He understood now why she'd looked at him the way she did then.

He sat looking back at her. Hell, his mouth was open; he must look a total dick. He shut it, so fast that his teeth clicked, and his father glanced at him.

A voice asked 'Ben Coles?' A guy, in a dark red top like the others, had come into the room; was gazing in their direction. Ben stared again. It was Jake, the shaven-headed nurse.

So why hadn't he recognised Ben? 'Hi, Ja—' Ben started to say, then realised that this man was a little older, a little shorter. But he had the same tough, strong build and the same gleaming head. *Far too much is happening at once*, Ben's mind told him.

His father stood up. 'That's us. This is Ben; I'm Matt.'

'Tim.' The guy shook Mr Coles' hand, then Ben's. 'Good to meet you. Like to come through this way?' He headed off towards the corridor, father and son following. Ben's father had moved to take the wheelchair handles, but Ben started pushing himself along.

He wanted the girl to see that he could do this. He hadn't looked in her direction again; didn't know if she was still watching him or not.

The nurse, doctor, whatever he was, stopped by a doorway a few metres down the corridor, and waved them in. Ben wheeled himself into a big, square room. A wooden rail ran along one wall, about waist height. The floor was partly lino, partly carpet. Sets of wooden steps, some just one tread high, others taller, stood against another wall. Pairs of metal crutches were arranged in a rack.

'Like to park yourself over here?' The guy — Tim — nodded to Ben and pointed to a desk beside the row of crutches. 'You want to pull up a chair?' he asked Mr Coles. 'Be good if you can see what's going on.'

He pulled up a chair himself, beside Ben, leaned forward and gazed at the stump with its elasticised bandage. 'I'm gonna be your prosthetist, buddy. We'll be seeing a lot of each other over the next weeks. Months, quite probably.' He straightened up; looked at son and father. 'My job is to see that the leg we give you is as efficient and comfortable as possible. You OK with that?'

'I — yeah.' Ben tried to concentrate on what the man was saying, but he kept thinking of the girl in the waiting room. What had happened to her hand? How long ago?

Somehow, she looked sort of used to the place, the way she was sitting with her phone.

'The first leg we do for you won't be for ever,' Tim was saying. Even his voice sounded like Jake's. 'They wear out. New and better ones come along all the time. Some of the latest ones even have built-in computers. Plus you're still growing, so we'll need to change the prosthesis as that goes on. No probs: that's what we're here for.'

He nodded at Ben's left leg. 'OK if I take a look?' As Ben said 'Yeah', the shaven head bent forward again, peeled back the stump-shrinker, and stared at the stump. 'That's looking real good. How long since it happened?'

Ben glanced at his dad, who said, 'Bit over two weeks.'

That long? thought Ben. OK, he'd been out of it for the first few days. At the same time, he was thinking, *Only two weeks?* Sometimes it seemed as if he'd been a — a cripple? Was that what he'd become? — for ever.

'Yeah,' The prosthetist was murmuring. 'Healing really well. Mr Dev's done a great job. Top guy.' He glanced up at Ben, and grinned. 'Demon squash player, too. Did you know?'

Ben blinked; shook his head. 'He thrashes me once a week,' Tim went on, and gazed again at the stump. 'You on painkillers much?'

It was Mr Coles who answered. 'Not since the first

few days. He's a brave young guy.' Ben felt his face grow warm.

'That makes it easier,' Tim said. 'Some medications affect the blood supply.' He was still bent over, studying the remains of Ben's left leg. 'Should have something ready for you to try on in a couple of weeks. Maybe less.'

'So I can't get the . . . the prosthesis now?' It came out as a challenge. 'Sorry, I just —'

'Nah. Sorry, mate. Gotta let your stump tissue mend as much as poss, till it can take the wear and tear. The new leg will rub against it, though we pad the residual limb with socks for the best fit. Plus there's the weight of your own body on it. Best not to hurry things. We'll try you on crutches till then. They're good practice for standing and moving around.'

He stood. 'Now, we want a pair that fit you nice and comfortably. Like to wheel yourself over here?' He moved towards the wooden rail running along one wall.

Ben trundled his wheelchair across. 'I need to check your height,' The prosthetist went on. 'Crutches are too short, you end up bent over like a chimp. Too long, you're on tiptoes. Can you face the rail here and haul yourself up? I'll hold you so you don't fall.' He turned to Mr Coles. 'Could you keep a hand on the chair so it doesn't go flying off?'

Ben gripped the rail, waited till he felt his father's hands on the wheelchair handles behind him, and pulled himself up till he was standing. His arm exercises were helping, he knew as he came upright, hopping a bit on his right leg.

'Great.' Tim picked up a tape measure from the table nearby. 'If you can just stay steady there for a minute —'

Ben felt his father move to support him; went, 'I can do it.'

Mr Coles stayed close as the prosthetist measured Ben's height — not from head to foot, but from elbows to foot, and then from stump to ground. 'Good. Now let your dad help, 'cos I'm gonna get you to keep standing up while we try these.' Tim reached across to the rack and took out a pair of crutches.

Ben's father put an arm around him, while the prosthetist tucked one crutch under Ben's left arm. 'Elbow goes into that leather socket there. Hold the rubber grip. That's it. How's it feel for length?'

Ben wasn't sure, but he said 'OK'.

'Looks pretty fair. Let's try the other side. You're gonna take both hands off the rail, but your dad's got you, remember, and you can lean on the first crutch.'

Mr Coles tightened his hold. Ben grasped the rubber handle in his left hand harder and let go of the rail.

Instantly, Tim slipped the other crutch under his right elbow.

'Got it? Great. Now, I want you to try a couple of steps. You do it in three stages, OK? First, stand as straight as you can. Then swing both crutches forward together and put them down firmly. That starts you leaning forward as well. Finally, you take a hop to catch up with the crutches. Let's take it one thing at a time. Ready? One — stand up straight.'

Ben realised he was breathing hard. He straightened his back; tried to make sure his right leg was in line with his body.

'Good. Now when you're ready, lift the crutches together, and swing them forward. Don't skid them, and not too far. OK, part two — swing forward.'

The crutches felt light but strong. They came off the ground easily. Ben swung them forward half a metre, thumped the rubber tips onto the ground, and leaned after them. His right leg shook slightly.

'Good. Not too far, eh? You're walking, not doing the long jump. Last part, number three. A bit of a hop. Not too much for that, either. Let your body weight carry you forward, so your foot lands between the crutches. When you're ready.'

Ben pictured it. Then he pushed with his right foot; felt

himself swing forward. He went further than he meant, and his right leg ended up between the crutches, but ahead of them, so he was leaning backwards. He began to topple, and immediately his dad grabbed him.

'Not bad at all,' Tim said. 'Like I say, keep the hopping short at first. You'll get used to it. Those crutches making you lean forward too much?'

'I — yeah, a bit.' Ben hadn't noticed till now.

'That's why you're taking a bigger hop than you need to. Let's try a longer pair. Couple of centimetres makes all the difference.'

The prosthetist drew another pair from the rack. One at a time, he took the crutches Ben was gripping; helped him fit his elbows into the other pair's leather sockets. His father kept holding him.

'OK, let's see you stand. That better?'

It was. Ben felt the difference straightaway. He stood more upright, felt more stable. 'Yeah. Great, thanks.'

'So let's try another step. Not too far, remember. One —'

Ben stood as straight as he could. 'Two —' The crutches lifted and swung forward. 'Three —' He leaned and hopped; landed neatly between the rubber tips. He swayed slightly, then stood upright. He knew there was a stupid grin across his face.

'Brilliant, buddy. Now sit and have a breather, then we'll go for a tramp.'

A tramp. The words took Ben back to the shingle slopes and boulders of Pangonui. His dad helped him back into the wheelchair, while Tim typed things into a screen on his desk. As his breathing slowed down, Ben thought again of the girl in the waiting room. Would she still be there?

Across the big square room Ben tramped — hopped and swung, anyway — about thirty more steps on the crutches. Every one was easier than those before. He did some on the lino, some on the strip of carpet. 'Any new surface, you go really short and slow for a start, OK?' Tim told him.

He tried climbing one of the sets of steps. Tried, but could hardly manage. He had to lift up and jab down the crutches; shove himself much harder to hop onto the higher step. Plus they were a lot narrower than the areas of floor. He'd have fallen almost every time, if Tim and his father hadn't been holding him.

'No worries,' The prosthetist told him. 'There's lifts and ramps and escalators in most places. Plus you'll get better. I'll check your stump, and we'll let you go. Excellent session, buddy.'

His stump: Ben had almost forgotten it. He sat breathing hard again in the wheelchair, while Tim ran the tape measure around his left calf, then took another look at where the stitches had been.

'Good, good. Practise with the crutches at home. Several times a day, on different surfaces. Have someone with you all the time, eh? Don't try too much at once. And keep that stump really clean; we don't want any infection at this stage.' Tim held out a card to Mr Coles. 'You can ring this number if there's any problem. Right — see you Friday.'

His father wheeled him back into the corridor. The other prosthetist came out of another room nearby, smiled at them, put her head into the waiting room, and called 'Maddie?'

As they reached the waiting-room entrance, two figures were in the doorway. Tessa — he remembered that old bloke had called her — and someone shorter with fair hair. 'Sorry to keep you waiting, Maddie,' The prosthetist was saying.

The girl went, 'No worries.' She saw Ben. They both looked at each other as his dad wheeled him on down the corridor. Then, as she turned in the other direction to follow the prosthetist, the girl gave him a smile.

SEVENTEEN

Maybe it wasn't really a smile, he thought as his dad drove him home. It might just have been the way she looked at him. Hell, why was he thinking about someone he'd seen only three times and never spoken to? Maddie: cool name. Actually, she looked pretty . . . well, sane to him. *He* was the one who sometimes got mad about things these days. He snorted, and his father glanced at him. 'Leg hurting, mate?'

Actually, it was. Practising with the crutches must have stirred it up. There was a stabbing in his vanished left ankle, and an ache in his vanished left foot.

But as soon as Mr Coles had pushed him up the ramp into the house, kissed Mrs Coles when she came out of the room she used for her polytech stuff, and headed off for The Great Indoors ('Time I sold someone a few couches'), Ben wheeled himself into the living room.

'Mum?' he called.

'Just a second, love,' came his mother's reply. 'Got to enter one more assignment grade.'

When she came through into the living room, Ben got her to hold the wheelchair while he tucked a crutch under each elbow and levered himself up onto his feet. He nodded towards the other end of the room. 'Stand there, Mum.'

'You sure, love? Do you need a —'

'Just stand there.' Ben edged the crutches closer to his body; made sure he was standing upright. He swung the crutches forward, thumped them down onto the carpet, swung himself after them, and brought his right foot down exactly between them. His mother stood, watching. Again: upright — crutches forward — swing and hop. And again, four times, till he was standing right in front of his mother, wobbling a fraction and grinning.

'Oh, love, that's marvellous! I'd forgotten how tall you are!' Mrs Coles hugged him (he wobbled a bit more), reached up, and kissed him on the cheek.

Ben had forgotten something, too. This was the first time since it happened that he'd been able to look someone straight in the eye. With Tim the prosthetist, he'd been concentrating too much on the crutches to notice, but suddenly he didn't have to stare up at people, the way he had from hospital bed and wheelchair. He was equal with them. He could even look down on them a bit, like he was doing now with his mum. It made him feel like he had before . . . before his life changed forever.

He did exercises that afternoon. He did a bit more schoolwork, too. Not too much: Mrs Sione would let him off because of his leg, he decided. He moved around the house from rooms with carpet to rooms with bare board to rooms with lino, practising smaller steps on the harder, more slippery surfaces. His arm muscles started to grumble, but it was so good to stand and walk. Stand and hop, anyway. He felt good. Sore, but good. His mother kept checking on him, and tried to look as if she wasn't.

At lunch, he swung himself to the table, got into the chair OK, placed the crutches on the floor beside him, and began pulling himself up closer to the table, to eat. His mother started hurrying around to help, and almost tripped over one of the crutches. Ben smirked at her.

'Don't rush things, Mum. Remember?'

When they'd eaten, he realised he couldn't carry dishes to the sink. He needed both hands on the crutches. 'I'll get my chair,' he announced. 'No, *I'll* get it.' On his crutches, he swung to where his wheelchair was parked in the living room, turned and let himself drop onto the seat, then clutched the arms as the chair shot backwards against the wall, leaving a black mark. Without telling his mother, he wheeled himself back into the dining room and put the dishes away — very carefully.

He slept OK that night. The stump-shrinker helped protect his leg in bed, while he seemed to have learned how to turn over without it catching and stabbing.

He thought about the girl with the missing hand. Maddie. Maybe she'd be there when he saw Tim on Friday. How would he feel about that? Actually . . . he wouldn't mind. She *had* smiled at him. He was sure of it. Almost.

Thursday. Hom came, checked blood pressure, pulse, heart, stump. 'All good. You are walking on the crutches?'

'*With* the crutches,' Ben said, then felt his face go hot.

'Sorry. Didn't mean to . . .'

Hom just laughed. 'English is a strange, strange language.'

Leg-lifting exercises, with the weights. Arm-lifting, also with the weights. 'You need strong arms for the crutches. And when your new leg comes, arms will help you walk.'

Ben grinned. 'I'm not gonna walk on my hands!' Then, 'Hom? When do you think I can go back to school?'

The physio was packing up her gear. 'Tim will say. Very soon, I think. You will enjoy your schoolwork — *on* the crutches and *with* the crutches!'

Friday morning. It hadn't been a very good night. His missing foot twinged and throbbed. Finally he put the light on, pulled himself up in bed, sat massaging and pinching all around the stump.

His mother drove him to the hospital. She'd taken his dad to work earlier. 'He's got a lot of stuff to catch up on.' Ben thought again of the ramp, the handles, the doors. *Mum and Dad are paying for all these?* he wondered once more.

As they entered the waiting room, Ben swinging along

on his crutches, he glanced all around. The old guy was there, but no sign of the girl.

They sat down near the old bloke. 'Morning, laddie,' he went to Ben. *Yeah, Scottish, all right.* He turned to Ben's mum. 'Angus Dalgliesh.'

'Beth Coles. Ben's showing me around.'

Blue eyes under bristly white brows looked at Ben. 'You'll do fine. Young ones can learn to handle anything. You should see Maddie tapping away on that iPhone contraption of hers.'

Mrs Coles looked puzzled. 'Maddie?'

'Fine little lassie who comes here. Artificial hand — been like that for ever.'

'You know her, Ben?' He shrugged, pretended not to be interested. But he was thinking: *Been like that for ever. So how did . . .?*

He and his mother spent the best part of an hour with Tim. The shaven-headed prosthetist got Ben to walk around the room on his crutches. He got him to try the steps again, holding him from the side, and Ben managed to climb up three of them OK, though when he shuffled around, he hadn't a clue how to start coming down again. 'We'll try that next week,' Tim told him.

Then he sat while his stump was checked and measured. 'Really good,' The prosthetist nodded. 'Hardly any fluid at all. We can take that stump-shrinker off now, I reckon.'

He peeled the elastic bandage away. Ben saw his mother biting her lip as the severed flesh and folded skin was revealed. 'No raw patches,' Tim announced. 'No sign of ulcers. Hadn't expected any, but that's good, too.' He produced a pair of thick, wide black socks. 'Want you to wear one of these all the time on the residual limb till I see you on Monday, buddy. Just to remind you to be careful. Wash it every day, will you? Like I say, gotta watch the hygiene.' He grinned at Mrs Coles. 'Ben does all the washing and ironing, I presume?'

They headed down the corridor again. Ben made sure he was moving upright and smoothly as they passed the waiting room. But there was just one woman waiting in it, in a wheelchair. No Angus. No girl.

Been like it for ever, he thought again. He tried to think what must have happened to her as a baby, and shuddered.

EIGHTEEN

'What was that girl's name? The one Angus mentioned?' his mother asked on the way home. 'Maybe she can tell you what it's like with . . . when you have a prosthesis.' Ben grunted.

The rest of Friday dragged past. Saturday *crawled* past. A text from Manu said he was helping his dad and his uncles at the marae, but hey, could he drop in on Sunday? A text from Connor said he had Taekwondo in the morning and had to visit his aunt and her partner in the afternoon (*boring as, bro*), but hey, could he drop in on Sunday? And had Manu told him about this soccer thing coming up?

His dad was at The Great Indoors. His mother was vacuuming. He'd even do a stink job like that, if he could.

He made himself start some exercises; gave up halfway through. What was the use? Schoolwork? Yeah, nah. Connor's text about a *soccer thing*: all right for his mates, but he — Ben — wouldn't ever be playing again.

Aunt Josie and Uncle Kyle arrived in the afternoon. Ben thought of Connor's text; *he* wouldn't care how boring people were, as long as he could just go out whenever he wanted and see them.

His uncle watched as Ben swung himself around on his crutches; said, 'Good stuff, mate. That'll give your mum and dad something to smile about, for a change.' So Ben tried to seem a bit more cheerful while they were there. It helped — a little.

He slept OK. The sock Tim had given him (it looked like a thick woollen bag with an elastic top) made his stump feel more protected. And getting out of bed was easier now. Instead of having to struggle sideways and down into the wheelchair, he could reach for his crutches where they stood against the wall, fit them under his elbows, and lever himself up onto his feet. His foot, anyway. So he started Sunday feeling more hopeful.

He got to the bathroom, lowered himself onto the high loo seat easily enough, and turned on the shower when he'd finished. As he wriggled out of his undies and T-shirt, his elbow sent a crutch clattering to the floor. Two seconds later, his mother was calling from behind the curtain across the bathroom doorway. 'Ben?'

'I'm OK. Knocked a crutch over, that's all.'

'You want me to —'

'No! I'm getting in the shower. I'm all right!'

He heard his mother sigh as she moved away.

His parents were eating breakfast. Ben swung into the dining room on his crutches, then paused. 'I want to try something. Dad, can you be ready?'

As Mr Coles stood, Ben leaned both crutches against the wall, steadied himself with one hand for a second, then set off, hopping across the room on his right leg, heading for the table. His dad moved towards him; his mother half-rose. Ben reached the table, grabbed the edge, and lowered himself onto a chair, puffing slightly. 'See?'

'Well done, buddy,' his father went. 'But don't rush it, remember.'

Inside his head, Ben muttered several rude words. When were people gonna stop saying that to him?

Connor and Manu arrived together about 10.30. Ben was sitting on the living-room couch, where his mother had just finished massaging the olive oil and Vitamin E cream onto his stump.

'Hey, bro' . . . 'Hi, bud,' They greeted him, then gazed at his stump. Rather, Manu gazed; Connor looked as if he was trying not to see it. 'Like I say, that's amazing, bro,' went Manu. 'Incredible they can just sew it up like that.'

'Yeah.' Ben liked the way Manu talked about the injury. He didn't fuss; didn't exaggerate. He just told it like it was.

Connor, meanwhile, was making himself look properly. 'Hurt much?'

'Only when I'm running a marathon. Hey, what do you guys want to do?'

Manu grinned. 'Thought we might take you out and do some more wheelies, like last time. Might run into those girls again.'

Ben nodded. 'Cool. But not in the wheelchair.

On these.' He was already fitting the crutches under his elbows, starting to heave himself off the couch.

'You sure?' went Connor. 'We can —'

'Sure I'm sure. Come on. Can you tell Mum and Dad, Manu?'

He was nearly at the side door with its ramp, when his parents appeared from the dining room. 'Ben, what are you doing?' his mum asked.

'We're just going out for a bit. I'll be all right.'

His father was frowning. 'Use the chair, eh, buddy?'

But Ben was already at the ramp leading down to the path. 'I'll be OK! I can handle it.'

He turned away from his parents. 'Hey, what's this soccer thing you texted about, Connor?'

Connor glanced at Manu, who looked awkward. 'No big deal. Some coach coming along to talk to us.'

Talk to you, maybe, Ben thought. *Not to me any longer.* He swung his crutches forward, faster than he meant to, leaning after them as they thudded down onto the wooden slope. Too late, he realised that the downward angle meant he was bending much further forward. He made an awkward half-hop on his right leg, tried to land it between the crutches. But the force of his swing took him way past; the crutches slewed sideways behind him, and next second he was plunging forwards and down, towards the concrete of the path.

He heard his mother cry out. Manu leapt, half-grabbed his shoulder. Ben managed to get one hand in front as he collapsed onto the path. His forehead and one cheek scraped across the pitted surface, and he grunted with shock. His lower body buckled and thumped onto the ramp.

Voices were shouting. 'Ben!' . . . 'Jeez!' . . . 'Buddy!' He could taste blood in his mouth. Aw, hell, he'd smashed some of his teeth after all.

For a few seconds, it was like being up on the maunga all over again. He sprawled face down; his father arrived beside him, crouching and staring. 'I told you to — no, stay still!' Manu and Connor were gaping down at him. His mother stood, hands pressed to her face.

'The leg —' Ben gasped. Mr Coles was already moving his son's lower body gently on the ramp. 'I think it's OK. You fell with the right leg underneath. For God's sake, mate, what were you trying to do?'

His nose and forehead were grazed. His bottom lip had a cut where it had been squashed against his teeth — his still-there teeth. His right palm was scraped and bleeding. But his stump seemed OK.

He stayed sitting on the concrete path while his

mother washed his grazes with a facecloth. Connor shook his head. 'Hell, bud, you scared the crap out of us. Sorry about the language, Mrs C.' Ben's parents said nothing.

But after Ben had been lifted into the wheelchair and pushed back up into his room, and the sock removed to check his stump was undamaged ('Lucky, eh, bro?' Manu said. 'You better buy a Lotto ticket'), and after his friends had stayed for a bit and then left, Mrs Coles came into the room, pulled its curtain closed behind her, and gazed at her son.

'If you ever do anything like that again, Ben Coles, I'm going to smack your bottom. Ben, dear, you could have hurt yourself so badly. I know you're in a hurry to get back to being . . . being you. But you could have split that stump open, ended up back in hospital. You hear me, love?'

Ben sat staring at the duvet. 'Yeah. Sorry, Mum. I stuffed up.'

His mother rested a hand against Ben's cheek. 'You're doing so well, love. But be careful. For your sake and everyone's. Think about it.' She went out, leaving Ben to do just that.

'No downhill slaloms, remember,' Ben's mother told him as he and his dad left for the hospital on Monday morning. 'I've got too many assignments to finish marking. Can't keep rushing out to pick you up.' She leaned forward after he'd got himself into the car and ruffled his hair. 'Aw, Mum!' Ben protested.

His father was going to take him to the waiting room, then head off to work and come back later. 'You OK to wait there, buddy? You're a veteran of those places now.'

'No worries. Thanks, Dad.' His father re-ruffled his hair.

The two of them headed along the familiar corridor, Ben swinging himself along steadily but carefully on his crutches. Nobody else was in the waiting room. No girl. No old guy. Mr Coles checked with Reception, then headed off. Ben quickly combed his hair. But when Tim appeared, three minutes later, Ben was still the only one in the room.

The shaven-headed figure in his dark-red tunic gazed at the grazes on Ben's nose and forehead. 'Been skydiving?'

Ben shrugged. 'Been an idiot.' He described what had happened on the ramp. Tim nodded; said nothing. He pointed to a chair, waited till Ben sat, then peeled off the black sock. 'Stump looks good. That's the main thing. Right — let's start talking about your new leg.'

'First fitting next week, maybe,' Tim told him. 'There'll be a lot of sessions, buddy. We want to make sure it's really comfortable.'

Ben stood as straight as he could, while the prosthetist again measured his height; length of right leg; length from hip to knee and knee to stump on the left leg. He got Ben to take off the sneaker and sock from his right foot, ran the tape measure along his right foot and around his ankle, even wrote down the length of Ben's toes.

'The prosthesis is gonna feel heavier than your own leg did. They make them out of carbon fibre and high-strength plastic compounds, but they still feel more bulky for a while. Opposite to what you are now, so you'll have to sort out your balance all over again. OK?'

As Ben nodded, Tim went on. 'Really important thing is gonna be looking after your stump. Half your body weight will be pressing down into the prosthesis. Like I say, we make the fit as perfect as we can, plus we pad the socket and stump. But any redness, soreness, you tell us straightaway. Worst thing that can happen is ulcers on the skin, so washing, and using that Vitamin E cream — they both stay really important. Questions so far?'

'When can I go back to school?'

Tim laughed. 'You're keen! Thought you might like a long holiday. Nah, getting back to ordinary stuff as soon as you can is a good idea. End of this week, if you feel up to it. Wheelchair for the first few days —' He saw the expression on Ben's face. 'I know. The crutches make things faster, but wait till you've sussed stuff out at school. There'll be slopes and steps you never noticed before. You saw what happened when you tried to be too quick with things.'

Ben said nothing. 'Might be a good idea to do a recce, a day or so before you go back,' The prosthetist went on. 'Get someone to take you down, wheel yourself around and take a look. Schools can usually help if there's issues with access and stuff. Don't hesitate to ask, eh?'

He watched Ben for a second. 'You're making real progress, buddy. Once you're used to the new leg, you'll be able to do heaps of stuff. Just be careful and keep working at it. Plenty of exercises with those weights, eh? Build up your strength. How about we aim for school on Thursday? Then when you come here on Friday, we can see if there've been any issues. OK, go for it — slowly.'

As he swung himself back towards the waiting room, Ben knew he was grinning. Grinning about going back to school! And about what Tim had said. *You'll be able to do heaps of stuff.* A surge of hope rose up inside him, so strong that he heard himself drag in a deep breath. He'd exercise with those weights as soon as he got home.

He came into the empty waiting room with the grin still on his face. It wasn't empty any longer. Angus sat looking at him. The girl sat watching, too.

'You look very cheerful, laddie,' Angus went. 'And you look like you've been headbutting your wheelchair.'

'Tried to go down a ramp. Ended up on the concrete path.' Ben hoped he sounded tough and cool.

'Aye, we all have accidents to begin with.' Angus watched while Ben manoeuvred himself onto a seat. The girl hadn't said anything. There was no sign of her red mitten. 'So — it's Ben, isn't it? Ben, meet Maddie. Maddie, meet Ben.'

'Hi.' . . . 'Hi.' A quick glance, then both looked away. Angus was still talking. 'Now, we're all in the same boat here. Want to tell us what happened with your leg, laddie? They always say it feels better if you can talk about it.'

Ben swallowed. The old guy's question had set his mind whirling. He hadn't actually spoken the words out loud up till now. 'I — I was tramping. On Pangonui, with my dad. Boulder fell on me. On my leg. Smashed the bones.' He paused, said, 'It was my fault. I tried to go the easy way, got myself into trouble.'

As he stopped, he realised Angus was right. Talking about it made him feel a fraction better. Made things clearer, more real. Maddie kept watching him.

Angus nodded. 'Aye, that's bad luck. But you're young and strong, and you'll get over it. They're great people here. In a while, you'll be able to do almost everything. Isn't that right, Maddie?'

The girl smiled. *Yeah*, Ben decided, *that's definitely the smile she gave me that other time. Well, almost definitely.*

He hadn't meant to say his next words; was startled when they came. 'How about yours? Your leg?'

Angus chuckled. 'Ah, it's nowhere near as exciting as your story. We're going back a long while, when I —'

He stopped as Tessa, the other prosthetist, appeared in the doorway. 'Kia ora, people. Ready for you now, Angus.'

Angus reached for his crutches and pushed himself up. *He leans a bit towards his missing leg side*, Ben noticed. *I might try that. Could help my balance, maybe.*

'Next exciting episode when I see you again, laddie. Ye'll have to hold your breath till then. Lead the way, Tessa.' He followed the smiling woman out into the corridor. Boy and girl were left alone.

NINETEEN

She — Maddie — was gazing at her phone. Neither of them spoke. Ten seconds. Twenty. Thir— Ben swallowed again. 'What did happen? To Angus, I mean?'

The girl didn't look at Ben. 'He used to work for an oil company. In Africa somewhere, way out in the jungle. Cut his foot on a sharp stone when he was having a shower outside.' She lifted her head, saw Ben staring, nodded. 'Sounds weird, eh? The cut got infected. By the time they reached a doctor, his foot had gangrene — was turning black and rotten. They had to take part of his leg off, too.' A pause. 'He's such a cool old guy.'

Her voice was quiet, steady. She began to look down at her phone again. If Ben's question about Angus had startled him, his next one amazed him. 'How about you? Your hand?'

She lifted her head again. 'Sorry, didn't mean to be . . .' Ben heard himself stammering. 'Just that he — Angus — said . . .' He trailed away. Hell, he must sound such an idiot.

The girl spoke in the same level voice. 'Congenital limb difference.' She watched Ben for a beat, began laughing as his mouth sagged open. 'Means I was born like that. Mum says I had a couple of tiny fingers on the end of the stump.' She raised her hand; gazed at it for a moment as if it belonged to somebody else. 'But they, like, didn't do anything; couldn't even move. The hospital took them off when I was about two, so they could fit a prosthesis better. I've worn one ever since then.'

Ben wasn't sure what to say. 'Does yours hurt?' he asked finally. 'I mean, the bit that isn't there. Does it sometimes feel like it's there?' Now he sounded such a *total* idiot.

Maddie shook her head. 'I was born without it, so my brain doesn't think it's there. That make sense?' When Ben nodded, she hesitated, then said, 'Must be, like, so unreal when you think you've still got it. Is *yours* sore?'

Now was the chance for him to be a big hero; say *I can handle it*, or something like that. Instead, Ben told her, 'I still get cramps and stuff, in my ankle mostly. And one time, my big toe got really itchy. I even reached down to scratch it, till I saw it wasn't there.'

The girl laughed, then looked embarrassed. 'Sorry, I know it's not funny. Not LOL funny, anyway.'

Another silence. This time she spoke first. 'When are you getting your prosthesis?'

'Tim reckons he'll start fitting it soon. This Friday. Maybe. He says it takes a while.'

The fair head nodded. 'They try to make it really perfect. I've had five hands, counting the first. Every three years or so, they make me a bigger one, 'cos I'm still growing. They'll keep doing that till I'm about twenty. Amazing, eh?'

'Yeah.' At the same time, Ben thought, *What's* really *amazing is that I'm talking away like this to a girl.*

'That's what I'm coming in for now,' she went on. 'My new one isn't gripping things properly, and Tessa is getting it fixed. I can wear the old one if I need to, but it's a bit tight. I use it for netball.' She grinned. 'Scares the other teams.'

'I bet.' Ben tried to think of something really cool to say. 'Can't wait to get my one — my prosthesis. I'm so over looking weird. I just want to look . . . well, normal.'

The moment he spoke the words, he realised what he'd done. Maddie's face went still. She watched him for a moment. 'You think I *don't* look normal?'

'No! No, I didn't mean that. I —'

'Hi, son. Sorry to keep you waiting.' His father was coming through the doorway. 'You ready to go?' Mr Coles nodded to the girl. 'Hello.'

She was bent over her phone again. She mumbled something to Ben's dad; didn't look up. All the way along the corridor into the car, and all the way home, Ben tried to understand how he could have been such a total, *absolute* idiot. He could kick himself — if it was possible to do that with just one leg.

He told his parents about going back to school on Thursday; about maybe having a recce first; about keeping up the exercises and looking after his stump. He didn't mention the girl Maddie, but all through the rest of Monday, he kept thinking what a total, absolute, *brainless* idiot he'd been.

Hom came on Tuesday; nodded when he mentioned school. 'After that, I perhaps see you less. But you can text me.' She checked his stump and ran through his exercises. 'Do them all. Keep squeezing your bottom.' Hell, he hoped nobody ever heard her saying that.

She watched while he walked around the room on his crutches. 'Tim says you fell over on the ramp. Let us see how you use it.' They moved to the side door. 'I stand below, so you are safe. Now — do not swing both crutches. Do a little step with one crutch, then the other. Be like a penguin walking. Make small hops after them and keep a little leaning back.' Ben's mother had come out of her office and stood watching.

It worked. He felt awkward at first, jerking downwards with one crutch after another. Like a robot, he decided, not a penguin. But he got down the ramp three times. Coming up again, he just had to lean further forward. 'Stop and think first,' Hom told him. 'Don't —'

'— Don't rush into things,' Ben and the physio went together. They and his mum all laughed. 'I will see you after your school on Thursday,' Hom said. 'You may be sore and stiff. But enjoy!'

When his mother drove him to school on Wednesday afternoon, half an hour after lessons ended, Connor and Manu were there waiting for him. 'Spending extra time in this place!' Manu shook his head. 'You owe us, bro!'

'You're good friends to him, you two,' Ben's mum said, and his mates looked embarrassed. 'Someone's gotta keep an eye on him, Mrs C,' Connor grinned. 'Can't trust him by himself.'

They took the wheelchair from the car, and Ben pushed himself from carpark to classroom to toilet to assembly hall. Yeah, Tim was right; he'd have been struggling on his crutches. But there didn't seem to be any major problems. There was even a ramp up to the hall, which Ben had never noticed before. The door into his form room looked a bit narrow, but he could manage, slowly. 'If there's a fire alarm, you go out the door,' Connor told him. 'The rest of us will already be out the windows.'

The three of them laughed. 'Don't worry, bro,' Manu said. 'Mrs Sione reckons the teachers have all worked out what to do.'

Mum's right, Ben knew. *These guys are good friends.*

They talked about his new leg. Manu asked if he could leave it outside the principal's door for a joke. Connor wanted to know if he'd seen anyone at the hospital with a prosthetic head, and Ben's mother exclaimed, 'You boys!' Ben told them about Tim and Angus. He didn't mention Maddie, but he kept thinking about her. What could he say to her next time, to make up for his stupid *weird* effort? Would she even listen to him? He slept poorly that night.

When his dad turned the car into the school carpark on Thursday morning, quarter of an hour before the bell, his mates were waiting for him again. 'Knew you'd get lost by yourself,' Connor told him. Manu went, 'Don't forget to leave a tip for your bodyguards.'

'Good luck, buddy,' Mr Coles told him as he drove off. 'You'll be fine. Text if there's any problem.'

Kids from different classes walked past. They all stared. A few quickly glanced away when Ben looked back. Two girls watched from over by the assembly hall corner; one of them said something that sounded like 'Oooh, yuck!' and Ben felt his face go hot. He glared in their direction and they moved away. Did they think he was — was weird, or something? They were the ones acting weird.

But then a couple of guys from his class called, 'Hey Ben, do a wheelie for us?', while another said, 'Watch out! It's Speed Demon!' Ben grinned at them, and felt heaps better. And three Year 11 girls smiled at him, going, 'Hello, Ben' . . . 'Hi Ben.' Manu shook his head. 'They think you're a super-hot guy now or something? Weird!'

'You're jealous, boy,' grinned Ben. Actually, he wouldn't mind if his mate was — a bit.

'Let's do a tour around the library block,' Connor said, as the bell for Form Time rang. 'We'll be late,' Ben told him, but Connor shrugged. 'Not a problem.'

So he pushed himself past the library, the science lab and the Food Technology room. Kids were heading inside; some just stared, but most of them went 'Hey, Ben' . . . 'Hi Ben', as well. Manu shook his head again. 'Next thing, they'll be asking for your autograph. Actually, do you know how to write, bro?'

By the time they reached the walkway to Room 11, everyone else had vanished. 'We're gonna be *really* late!' Ben said.

His friends glanced at each other, and Ben was sure they nodded. Then they took a handle of his chair each and started pushing him — fast — inside and along the corridor.

Someone was standing outside the classroom door. Mrs Sione. Aw, man, his first day back, and he was gonna get told off for being late. His mad mates . . .

Then his form teacher smiled. She stepped forward, placed a hand on his shoulder. 'Welcome back, dear Ben.'

She straightened up and smiled again. 'Come inside, then. You've got a lot of work to catch up on.'

Ben wheeled himself through the doorway, making sure he didn't scrape any paint off the sides. He glanced up, and all of his form class were watching him. Then they stood, everyone at once, and began clapping.

TWENTY

He'd never forget it. The guys were all grinning. A few of the girls held tissues, for some reason. The clapping went on, then it turned to laughing. Ben had turned his wheelchair to head for his usual place. The chair's arms rammed into two nearby desks; they and their seats toppled over, while folders, pens, books clattered and thumped onto the floor. 'Crasher Coles!' a voice yelled — Connor's, of course — while Ben tried to apologise in four directions at once.

He felt tired by the time he got home. Tired but good. There'd been a few issues he hadn't thought of. No way could his wheelchair fit under a school desk, so he'd had to park in the aisle and lean sideways — making sure he didn't topple — and do his work that way. He didn't mind; it meant he was closer to Neve and Miriana, two really cute girls in his class. They kept smiling at him, and he didn't mind that, either.

He was just so pleased to feel almost normal, though he still felt embarrassed about the way he'd last used that word. Next time he saw her — Maddie — he'd explain . . . somehow.

Connor and Manu stayed with him through the day. When he found there was a little half-step leading up into the library, they turned his chair around and hauled him up backwards, while six other guys also asked if he needed a hand. Connor wanted to know if the wheelchair had an eject button. 'You can go shooting up the steps, and we'll catch you at the top.'

A few kids stared or moved away if he came near. A couple more girls whispered to each other, until Ben looked hard at them. But nearly everyone said 'Hi' . . . 'Hey'. A few girls were almost *too* friendly: ones who'd never spoken to him before. It felt like they were putting on an act of how kind they were.

His bum was sore by the time his mother picked him up. He hadn't spent so long in the wheelchair before.

And there was a different sort of pain in his missing leg, a cramping where the bottom of his calf muscle used to be. He told Hom, who arrived soon after he got home, and she said, 'This is usual. Your brain thinks you are using those parts, and it still tries to send signals. Exercises help.'

So she took him through everything, from arm-stretching with weights to leg-lifting with slightly heavier weights than last time. He felt shattered by dinner time; pulled himself into bed early and slept hard. He was still stiff in the morning. But it was a good stiffness.

He changed the big black sock on his stump on Friday morning. His mum had washed the other one.

His father drove him to the hospital, before heading off to The Great Indoors once more. 'Be back to pick you up, buddy.'

Ben had told his mates he wouldn't be at school till lunchtime. 'Hell, wish I was you!' Connor exclaimed, then stopped suddenly. 'Sorry, wasn't thinking.' Manu thumped him on the arm, said, 'Connor *can't* think. Hey, anything we can do, bro, just say.'

Nobody in the waiting room. He felt half-relieved,

half-disappointed. Tim appeared. Ben swung himself along on his crutches to the usual room, and manoeuvred his way into a chair with arms that the prosthetist pointed to. Lots more movements were easier now.

Tim ran a tape measure around Ben's stump. 'Still no swelling. That's really good, especially after a day in the chair. School go OK?' When Ben said yeah, Tim turned and picked up something from a bench nearby. 'OK, here's the start of your leg.'

In the prosthetist's hands was a pinkish, plastic-looking shape like a narrow, deep bowl. From the other end, there stuck out a long metal rod that ended in a rubber stopper like one of his crutches. He swallowed. 'That's it?'

Tim grinned. 'That's part of it. The proper foot and all the fancy bits come later.' He tapped the bowl shape. 'First, we start getting a really good fit into the socket.'

The bowl had a lining of what looked like thick white mesh. 'It's called interface material. Made from polymers and silicons and other fancy-sounding stuff. Helps protect your stump, and the socket; gives us the best fit possible.'

He pulled another chair up beside Ben, and draped several socks like the one already covering his stump across it. 'Plus we use however many of these we need, to help.'

Ben was gazing at the socket. 'How does it stay on?'

Tim grinned. 'Sellotape. Nah, if we get a good tight fit, you get a sort of vacuum effect, and it mostly looks after itself. That's why we make the socket really deep. Plus there's an elastic bandage, like the stump-shrinker you had, except it's much wider, goes over the socket and up your residual limb. Really effective and doesn't squeeze too much. Your leg won't fly off if you're doing karate kicks — promise.'

He pulled up a low stool in front of Ben, and pushed a higher one towards the missing leg. 'Right, here we go. I'll get you to rest your stump on this. There's gonna be a bit of pushing and pulling, so hold on to the chair arms if you're feeling off balance. And speak up if there's pain, right? Shouldn't be any, but pain usually means a bad fit, and that's no use to either of us. So don't try and tough it out.'

He peeled back the black sock, peered at Ben's stump, then rolled the sock into position again. He took one of the other socks draped over the chair and rolled that on as well. 'That'll be too loose, probably, but let's see.'

Ben's left leg lay across the higher stool. Tim took the socket with its metal rod and slid the bowl shape carefully over the stump and socks. It covered his lower leg up to just a few centimetres below the knee. 'Comfortable?'

Ben nodded.

'We'll try the elastic bandage later,' said Tim. 'When things look a bit more snug. OK, can you lift that left leg and hold it up for me? Prosthesis doesn't weigh much yet.'

Eyes fixed on the socket, Ben raised what had been his leg. It came up easily; his weights had certainly helped. For a moment, real leg and metal rod stuck straight out in front of him. Then the prosthesis began to sag slowly.

'Bit loose, like I thought. You can lower it now.'

When Ben's stump was back on the stool, Tim removed the bowl and rod from it, picked up another sock from the chair, and fitted it on top of the other two. 'That'll start getting us closer. And now comes the really special piece of medical equipment I didn't tell you about.' He turned to the bench again, picked up something, and turned back.

Ben knew his eyes were bulging. Why? Tim was holding a tube of lipstick.

TWENTY-ONE

The prosthetist chuckled. 'Always enjoy doing that, sorry. You've met Angus? Tessa thought he was gonna have a coronary when she waved one of these at him.' He placed the lipstick on the chair beside him and began peering at the inside of the socket.

'We're not turning you into a fashion model, don't worry. This stuff is really useful. You'll see.' He picked up the lipstick again, and while Ben kept staring, he began drawing a series of stripes on the mesh inside the socket, from the rim down to the bottom of the bowl.

'Like I say, we want as snug a fit as possible. I'll put the leg back on, get you to slip your own leg into it, waggle it around a bit, and we'll see if the lipstick has rubbed off evenly. Make sense?'

Ben nodded. *Man, that's a relief,* he thought. He held the corners of the chair while Tim worked the lipstick-smeared socket (lipstick and bottom-clenching: *two* things he wasn't going to tell anyone about) onto his residual leg again. 'Just leave the leg on the stool this time, and move the stump around a bit inside the socket. Can you do that?'

Tim held the artificial half-leg while Ben shifted his own half-leg. Things did feel a tiny bit looser in some places and tighter in others. 'Fine,' said Tim after half a minute. 'That'll do.' He eased prosthesis from stump and gazed inside the socket.

'See?' He held it up to Ben. Yeah, a couple of places on the mesh still had almost untouched stripes. In a few others, the lipstick had vanished completely, while elsewhere it was evenly smeared.

Tim began marking areas with a highlighter pen. 'Bit of shaving off here; bit of building up there. No problem. Let's do it once more.'

The second try showed almost exactly the same marks. Tim nodded. 'I'll get to work on these and we'll try again on Friday. Like I say, it'll take a while, but it's worth it. Good start, buddy.'

As Ben was tucking his crutches under his elbows, he said, 'Meant to tell you. There's a guy in another part of the hospital who looks exactly like you. He's —'

The prosthetist grinned. 'He's called Jake. My little brother.'

So much going on, Ben thought again as he swung himself back along the corridor. Tim, Jake, Hom, Mr Dev: he'd have to start making a list. He was so busy picturing them all that he blinked as he came into the waiting room and saw two more faces he recognised. Angus and the girl. Maddie.

There was something different about her. It took him half a second to realise; then he saw she was wearing the red mitten again, on her right hand. She sat with head down over her phone; said nothing.

Angus was already speaking. 'Hello, laddie. How was today's session? Things coming along?'

'Tim started fitting the socket,' Ben told him, and saw Maddie look up. 'Amazing.'

Angus chuckled, and his bristly eyebrows rose. 'So ye'll have had the dreaded lipstick test, then? When Tessa showed me, I tried to tell her the colour was all wrong for my skin tone.'

The girl giggled. Ben saw that over her right wrist,

above the red mitten, was an elastic bandage, like the one that would help hold his leg on when he got it.

'Maddie says she's told you how I ended up with my piece of engineering.' He nodded at his stump. 'She and I are both waiting for our new, rocket-science models, then we'll be out on the town. Eh, lassie?'

The girl smiled. 'I couldn't keep up with you, Angus.'

'So how are you managing, Ben, lad?' The old man asked. 'Handling things OK?'

Ben nodded. 'Guess so. Went back to school yesterday.'

'Oh, aye. And how did that go?'

'Pretty good. Everyone wanted to help. Almost everyone, anyway.'

'Some of them won't even look, eh?' It took Ben a moment to realise Maddie was talking to him. 'And some make a big fuss about it — want to make themselves feel good.'

'Yeah, that's right.' So he wasn't the only one it had happened to. 'My mates are really cool, though; treat me like I'm just . . .' He glimpsed the danger word ahead; tried desperately to think of a different one, '. . . just the same.' A faint grin flickered across the girl's face, and Ben felt sure she'd guessed what he was about to say. Aw, hell! Wouldn't he *ever* stop looking like an idiot?

'You *are* the same, laddie,' went Angus. 'We've got to

keep remembering that. And we're better off here than in some places. When I got my first bionic leg, there were some countries where they didn't want me in restaurants, or where people moved their kids away from me in the street, like I had a disease or something.' He shook his head. 'Some folk are right daft.'

Ben didn't know what to say. Then Tessa the other prosthetist appeared. 'Mōrena, Angus. Ready to try your new mechanical miracle? We'll have you out and partying in no time.'

'Can't wait, lassie.' Angus levered himself up onto his crutches, stood still for a second, nodded to the boy and girl. 'Look after yourselves, you two.' He swung out of the room.

Now it was just the two of them once more. Ben took a breath, said, 'You're right. He's a cool old guy.'

'Yeah, he is.' Maddie began to gaze down at her phone. Ben swallowed, then went on. 'Look —' Her head came up at the word. 'I didn't mean what I said last time. That *normal* and *weird* stuff. I just wasn't thinking. Sorry.'

The girl half-shrugged. 'No worries.' She hesitated. 'And it's true sometimes, isn't it? People do look at you like you *are* weird or something.'

Ben remembered the ones who'd whispered and turned away at school. 'Yeah, they do.' He pointed at the red mitten. 'That your new hand?' Man, would she bite his head off again?

But she just held the hand up. 'Yeah. Got it yesterday. They'll keep checking it for a couple of weeks; make sure everything's, like, working. Feels heaps better than the old one.'

'Looks good,' Ben told her. It was true; except for the mitten, it looked almost normal. (Even inside his head, that word sounded dangerous.)

Maddie grinned again. 'They've even given me a manicure.' Ben saw the neat red ovals. 'I'm the only girl at our school who doesn't get told off for having them.'

She pushed back her hair — with the prosthetic hand. Ben heard himself speak yet another sentence he didn't know he was going to. 'What's the mitten for? Sorry: not trying to be nosy.' *I'm having a real conversation with a real girl*, he told himself again.

'It's while I'm getting used to the new hand. Reminds me to be especially careful. Mum's idea; won't need it for ever.'

Another figure appeared in the waiting room doorway. 'Hey, buddy,' Mr Coles said. 'You ready to go?' He nodded to Maddie. 'Hi, there.'

The girl murmured something and began looking at her phone once more. Ben pushed himself up onto his crutches, jerking his head as his dad began stretching out a hand to help. When he'd almost reached the door, he said, 'See you.'

Maddie lifted her head; went 'See you' back. Ben swung on down the corridor. When his father asked, 'That girl in for a prosthesis, too?' he just muttered, 'Yeah, suppose so.' But he felt good. No, he felt *really* good.

And that night, he walked on two legs.

TWENTY-TWO

It was so easy. He moved along the path between the library and his classroom block like he was walking on clouds. The concrete under his feet felt soft, even warm. He didn't have to make any effort; his legs carried him along smoothly, perfectly.

His class and others were watching and clapping, just like on his first day back. Incredible to think he'd worried about never being able to walk again — he was doing it better than he'd ever done in his life. He could run and jump if he wanted to; he felt sure of it. The people watching had begun calling out, telling him how brilliant he was.

Then he heard the words they were shouting. 'Weirdo! . . . What a freak! . . . One-legged wonder!'

One . . .? He glanced down, and they were right. His left leg from the shin down had completely vanished. His other leg was trying to carry him along, but there was nothing on the other side, and any second now he was going to fall. He couldn't stop himself. He saw the stump swing forward; his weight started to come down on it. Next moment, he was collapsing towards the concrete. He tried to shove his hands out, protect himself, but his arms were locked stiff. The stump of his left leg was plunging straight down at the hard ground.

He heard himself half-yell. His hands moved finally; clutched at the grass. No, not the grass: the sheets of his bed. He was lying on his back, gasping and shuddering. His heart raced; his body jerked.

Someone was still yelling at him. 'Ben? Are you all right, son?' His mother's voice, calling out from their bedroom. He tried to answer; made a croaking sound; managed to say, 'Yeah. Yeah, I'm OK. Just a bad dream.'

He hardly spoke at breakfast on Saturday, only grunted when his mother asked what his bad dream was about.

'Connor or Manu coming round?' his mum asked. Ben shrugged. His father said, 'I can always drive you over to one of their places, buddy,' and he shrugged again. His parents glanced at each other; said nothing.

His dad left for work, talking quietly to Ben's mother in the hall just before he drove off. Ben didn't try to help with the breakfast dishes. Instead, he swung himself into the living room, flopped down on the couch in front of the TV, and sat staring at its blank screen. He heard his mother moving around in her office.

After maybe quarter of an hour, she came into the living room, too, and sat down opposite him. Ben didn't look at her. Ten . . . twenty seconds passed, then his mum said, 'Sorry you're having a bad day, darling.'

Ben kept staring at the blank TV. His mother spoke again. 'Things won't ever be the same, will they, love?'

She was watching him steadily. 'You know it, son. Your father and I know it. Everyone does. But all of us — *all* of us are trying to help you, every way we can. You're grieving, darling. You've lost something precious; you feel depressed and sad. What we want to do — and that includes you — is to try and find ways through it.'

His mother smiled. A tired smile, Ben saw again. 'Been a while since I gave you a good nagging, hasn't it? Everything's hard for you just now, love. But remember — you've got a whole life in front of you still. Things are going to get better. So many people are doing things to make that happen. Your dad and I just want to do anything *we* can do to help, all right?'

Ben remembered Angus saying how young people could handle anything. He took a deep breath. 'Sorry. I know I'm being a pain. I just feel so useless, sometimes.'

To his surprise, his mum smiled. 'Well, you're definitely not useless. Your dad and I know that, and you'll find out in about . . .' She glanced at her watch. 'In about an hour.'

Ben blinked. 'An hour? What? Where? How?'

His mother smiled again. 'Wait and see. And now — now you can go and make your bed.'

He did. If he leaned on one crutch, he could straighten up sheets and duvet with his other hand. Tucking things in was still hard; he had to grip the bed sheets to keep his balance. He picked up the pillows — he was much better at reaching down now, provided he could hold on to something — and put them on.

Then he got the weights from by his bedside table, sat on a chair and worked through his exercises, doing some extra leg lifts. *You'll find out . . . about an hour.* What was his mother on about? He checked his watch. It was almost time — for what?

His mum appeared in the doorway. 'I'd better look at your leg, dear. It's healed so well, I almost forgot it.' She rolled the sock down carefully. 'Looks perfect. You want to see?'

'OK.' But as his mother left the room, Ben thought, *Perfect? I'll never . . .* He tried to shove the thought away as Mrs Coles returned, carrying a little hand-mirror. 'If I hold this, can you see the bottom of your stump?'

Ben peered down. 'Bit left . . . Hold it there.' He gazed, and kept gazing. He'd never seen the entire surface of the stump like this before. His residual limb ended in a gently rounded surface of skin. All sign of the stitches had vanished; only a couple of faint red scars ran across it. *It looks like . . . like my elbow*, he thought, *only bigger*. A sort of smooth knob, ordinary and weird at the same time. Nothing special, yet it had changed his whole life.

Tyres in the drive. His mother stood. 'Time for you to help your dad.' As Ben started to speak, she laughed. 'No, I'm not telling you. You'll find out soon enough.'

Mr Coles came into the room. 'Where's my new worker?' He saw his son's face, and laughed, too. 'Ready to join the payroll, buddy?'

In the car, Ben's dad talked about the weather, the traffic, how Uncle Kyle and Aunt Josie planned to drop in tomorrow. They swept into the parking lot behind The Great Indoors. Ben's father held the car door and then the shop's back door open (*I've got to learn how to do that for myself*, Ben thought) as his son swung himself through on his crutches.

The furniture store seemed to have a lot of new stuff: couches and chairs, especially. Rajan and Nikki, the two assistant managers, grinned as he appeared. 'Hey, Ben, great to see you!' . . . 'Don't let your old man work you too hard!'

His father pointed to the new chairs and sofas. 'Right, mate, you're our product tester. Your job is to sit on these, move around on them, decide how comfortable they are, and especially what it's like getting up out of them. A lot of our older customers want to know stuff like that. Give each thing a mark out of ten. Got your phone? Build up a list, and text it to me.'

Ben found he was grinning. Wait till he told Connor and Manu about this. For the next sixty . . . ninety minutes, he moved from chair to couch to recliner, sitting, bouncing and lying back on them, finding which ones he needed to haul himself out of, and which ones he could easily push up from. Most were comfortable; just a couple felt like they'd been designed by professional torturers.

Customers came and went, looked surprised or amused, made jokes about having the perfect job. When Ben had finished, his father handed him an envelope. Ben could see a couple of banknotes inside. 'Thanks, mate. That was really useful for us. *You* were really useful.'

Ben texted Manu and Connor: *U 2 slacking? I'm earning.* And he grinned as his father drove him home.

TWENTY-THREE

His two friends came round that afternoon. 'We're going to Burger Land,' Ben announced.

His mother smiled. 'That's fine, boys. But Ben — wheelchair, please.'

'It's only three blocks! I can get there.'

Mrs Coles shook her head. 'I know you can get there. But then you've got to get back. So — wheelchair, please.'

Ben muttered under his breath, but he knew she was right. And it didn't matter much, anyway, because outside Burger Land, they met Miriana and Neve, the two girls from his class. They talked and giggled to the boys, especially Ben. Halfway through, he realised what was happening. The girls wanted to make him feel good, but they were also trying to show how nice they were. OK, they *were* nice, but . . . well, he preferred the way Maddie spoke to him, no fuss and straightforward. What a weird thing to think.

'You see anyone our age in the hospital?' Neve asked.

'Yeah,' Ben told her. 'There's this girl Maddie with a prosthetic — an artificial — hand.'

Straightaway, the others started asking questions. 'What happened to her?' (Miriana); 'What school does she go to?' (Neve); 'She cute?' (Manu and Connor). So Ben gave them the same answer he'd given his father. 'She's just having something done to the hand.'

As they wheeled him back home, Connor said, 'Manu tell you about that soccer coach coming to school the other day?'

Manu cut in before Ben could answer. 'You didn't miss anything, bro. He just wanted to talk to anyone thinking about trying for pro teams later.'

Ben said nothing. *That could have been me*, he knew. His mum had told him how things would get better. *Not all of them will*, he thought now.

On Sunday morning, he remembered the homework Mrs Sione had set, remembered also the other work he hadn't done before he went back to school, and knew he should get started on that. *Nah, I'll do it later.* His teacher would let him off. He could always make out that his leg felt worse than it really was.

In fact, he hadn't been having too many pains. His missing ankle stabbed a few times; his vanished foot ached now and then. Weird little itches and twitches (hey, he was a poet!) ran through them sometimes. But he was getting used to it. And he didn't believe now that everything could magically reappear again. He still thought about what had happened nearly all the time, but he felt sad more than angry.

He didn't feel either of those on Sunday afternoon. Auntie Josie and Uncle Kyle arrived again, and this time they brought their seven-year-old twins, Millie and Margie. Then Connor and Manu wandered in. *They're so staunch, these guys*, Ben thought. He told them so: 'Knew you couldn't resist seeing someone with brains *and* good looks.'

The two little girls wanted a ride in the wheelchair. 'That's not for playing with, kids,' Aunt Josie told them. But Ben's mother laughed, and went, 'Ben's already banged it into enough doorways. They can't be any worse than him.'

So Manu and Connor pushed the twins along the

footpath, slow then fast, while Ben followed on his crutches, making police siren noises. Millie and Margie squealed, laughed, called, 'Watch us, Mummy, Daddy!' Mrs Bhatiani smiled from her front garden. *Weird*, Ben thought. *None of this would be happening if I were (Danger! Danger!) normal.*

'Hope your clothes fit over the prosthesis when you get it,' Ben's mother said as she drove him to school on Monday morning.

Ben looked down at his missing leg, and the flap of jeans that his mother had pinned up at the back. (Being the only guy allowed to wear jeans at school; that was a bit special.) *The prosthesis*: he was due to see Tim after school. Maybe it would be ready? A little shiver of excitement ran through him.

Some kids still looked uncertain when he came near, but most now treated him like they had before. Manu and Connor were ready to wheel him around, but he pushed himself as much as he could. Only the half-step leading up to the library was a problem. And his bum felt less sore: hey, maybe the clenching exercises were helping with that, too! But the sooner he could come to school on his crutches, the better. It made such a difference being able to look people straight in the eyes.

He'd never thought he'd enjoy doing lessons, but it felt so cool to be just doing the same as other people. *I should have finished that homework*, he thought. Oh well, he had his excuses ready.

It was after lunch (his mates had helped him into the library, and he'd had no trouble reaching down for books on the lower shelves) that Mrs Sione began talking with them about the work she'd set. Some kids had good answers; some had ordinary answers; some had awful answers.

'Ben?' Mrs Sione asked, so suddenly that he jerked. 'What did you put for this one?'

'I —' The words came out clumsily. 'I couldn't . . .' He pointed at his leg. 'It was . . .' His teacher said nothing; kept looking quietly at him. Ben knew his face had turned red. After a few moments, Mrs Sione turned to one of the girls instead.

But when lessons finished for the day, and Ben began pushing himself towards the door — he could do it without knocking desks over now — she called, 'Ben? Could you spare me a minute?' To Connor and Manu, she said, 'Won't keep your passenger for long.' His friends headed out into the corridor.

Mrs Sione came over to where Ben sat in his wheelchair. 'Is your leg very sore now?'

Ben shook his head. 'A bit. I can manage, though.'

His teacher nodded, was silent for a second. 'But you can't manage your homework?' As Ben started stammering something, she interrupted. 'Must be hard, trying to handle school things when you've got so much else going on in your life. You've had a huge shock; I can understand if you feel that homework assignments are too much for you just now.'

Ben didn't know what to say. His teacher waited, then went on. 'Don't settle for second-best, will you, Ben, dear? You're a bright kid as well as a brave one. I know that school stuff might seem pointless when you've got all this to deal with.' She gazed at where his left leg ended. 'But don't let yourself down. Make what's happened to you a challenge. And just say if there's any way I can help.'

Ben stared at the floor, then nodded. 'Sorry, Mrs Sione.'

His teacher smiled. 'It's a pleasure having you in my English class, Ben Coles. I'm never going to forget you. Make sure you do things so that the rest of the class don't ever forget you, either.' She rested a hand on his shoulder. 'Now go and look after Connor and Manu.'

Ben trundled along the corridor to where his friends stood waiting. 'She just wanted to ask if the leg was hurting much,' he told them, truthfully. Half truthfully, anyway.

TWENTY-FOUR

Twenty minutes later, his mum parked in the mobility carpark, and Ben began getting his crutches from the back seat. He opened the car door himself, swivelling around in the seat, remembered when he couldn't try such a movement without needing that little wooden tray under his backside. He'd managed such a lot in these few weeks. Mrs Sione was right. He mustn't —

Something tore at his left foot. Claws seized it; ripped and wrenched. He clutched the car's door handle, yelled 'Aaah! Aaah!'

Instantly his mother was there, clutching his arm and staring. 'Darling, what happened? Did you knock your leg? Are you all right?'

The ripping and wrenching vanished as fast as it came. Only a throbbing remained where his left foot had once been. 'I'm — OK. Phantom pain. A real hard one.'

He drew a deep breath and began easing himself out of the car. How long till his stupid brain believed what had happened? Hom had said something about . . . twenty years, was it? Great. Not.

A woman about his mother's age was in the waiting room, someone he'd never seen before. Nobody else. Ben's mother spoke to her; Ben half-spoke. After just two minutes, a shaven head poked around the doorway. 'Hey, mate. Like to come along?'

Ben swung himself across the room. He was so used to the crutches now that he hardly noticed them. He followed Tim along and into the familiar room. As the prosthetist turned around, Ben stared, heard himself go 'Wha—?'

The face under the shaven head had an eye that was half-closed, and surrounded by a purple-black, swollen bruise. Tim saw Ben's expression and chuckled. 'A prosthetic leg kicked me. Nah, this is from Mr Dev. Told you he was a demon at squash, didn't I? Had a game with him on Saturday. He didn't just thrash me; he belted the ball so hard it shot off my racquet into my face. Never heard a surgeon apologise so much.'

He picked up the socket and its attached metal rod from the desk beside him. 'Sit yourself down, buddy. Let's see how things fit today.'

When Ben's left leg was up on the stool in front of him, the prosthetist took off the sock and examined his stump. 'Demon squash player and a gun surgeon. Skin and everything looks good. Now, I've been taking a few bits out of the socket and building a few bits up. We'll get it on and see how it feels. Tell me if any part rubs.'

He slid the sock back onto Ben's residual limb, added another, then slipped on the bowl with its interface of mesh. 'Lift the leg up, and we'll have a look.'

Ben raised his left leg. The socket and metal rod stuck straight out in front. 'Keep it like that for a bit, if you can.' Tim held a hand underneath to support Ben's thigh, and they both watched. The rod didn't sag or move.

'Looks snug. Feel OK?' Ben nodded. 'Yeah.' And the socket did feel good: firm and comfortable.

'I'm gonna get you to stand and move around on it for a bit. No crutches —' as Ben began reaching for them. 'I'll catch you if you start to fall. But I want your full weight on the socket, so we make sure it's as near perfect as we can get it.'

He took Ben's elbow; helped him stand. The metal rod with its rubber tip felt like one of his crutches, except . . . except he was standing by himself, on his own two legs. He realised Tim had let go of his elbow, realised also that his own face was split by a vast grin.

The prosthetist smiled, too. 'Cool, eh? Nothing like being on your feet. Now, I want you to stand there for a bit. Take the weight. Tell me if it starts to hurt at all. Hold your arms out sideways to help balance yourself. Weight on both legs. I've got you if you start to fall.'

Ben stood, wobbling a little, but feeling more and more confident. Tim moved slowly around him, gazing at where his leg fitted into the socket, one hand outstretched and ready to grab him if necessary. 'How's that?' he asked, after a while. 'Great!' Ben replied, and meant it.

'Just gonna see if it's pushing the skin up above it too much,' The prosthetist said next. He ran one finger around the stump, just above the rim of the socket. 'Seems OK. So keep standing like that for the next twelve hours.' He saw Ben stare and laughed. 'Make that the next couple of minutes. Think about how it's feeling. Can you move your leg inside the socket for me?'

Ben tried, but the prosthesis fitted too snugly. He shook his head. 'Can't, sorry.'

Tim grinned, and his swollen eye looked even more swollen. 'Trick question. People think I want the leg to move, so they try really hard. If it stays put, shows the socket's fitting nice and tight.'

He took Ben's elbow. 'Now you're gonna take a few steps. Lift the prosthetic leg like it's an ordinary one, just a bit, then move it forward and put it down. Don't rush. Remember we're wanting to see how the socket feels.'

Ben stood without moving for a second, still wobbling slightly. He lifted his leg and swung the metal rod forward. It was so light that he could feel himself starting to tilt to the right. Tim gripped his elbow and steadied him. The rod came down on its rubber end, and there was a soft pressure against his stump. 'Feels cool.'

Tim nodded. 'Now you step onto your right foot. Means the socket is taking nearly all your body weight while your right leg's off the ground. Try and decide how that feels.'

He did it — swung his real, right foot forward and placed it down on the lino. He could feel the push of his left leg into its socket as the weight came onto it. 'Still OK,' he told Tim.

'Good,' The prosthetist went. He grinned at Ben. 'You realise you've just walked by yourself?'

So he had. Awesome. Incredible.

He took another twelve . . . fifteen steps on the left leg; stood on it for thirty more seconds; did another ten steps. 'It's sort of pushing a bit just there.' He pointed to where the inside of his calf would have been, 'Otherwise feels really good.'

Tim was rolling off the socks. 'Wondered if I might need to shave some more from there. No probs. OK, lipstick time again. What colour do you fancy today?'

In fact, it was the same colour as last time. Ben wriggled his stump inside the socket, then stood on it for a few more times, with the prosthetist hardly holding him. When the socket came off, the red marks were spread evenly inside it, except for a patch at the right where they were hardly visible. 'Yep, fraction more off there,' The prosthetist murmured. 'Good stuff, mate. We'll try again on Wednesday morning, OK?'

'Can I start using crutches at school?' Ben asked. Tim nodded. 'Should be OK. Just don't go whacking anybody with them.'

'And don't you go getting whacked by any squash balls.' Ben heard the prosthetist chuckling behind him as he swung off down the corridor.

In the waiting room, his mum sat talking to the other woman. Ben noticed now that she — the other woman — had shortish, fairish hair. Actually, she looked a bit like . . .

'So you're Ben.' She smiled at him. 'I'm Bridget Yelich, Maddie's mum. She's been telling me about you.'

Ben mumbled something. 'How are the fittings going?' she — Maddie's mother — asked.

'Good. Takes a while, though.' Meanwhile he thought, *Been telling me about you.* What did that mean?

'They're so careful and thorough,' The woman said. 'You're in good hands.'

His mother and Maddie's mother told each other how wonderful it was to have met up again. (*Again?* Ben thought.) Then Maddie's mum said, 'Funniest thing is, I only came in to see about a parking sticker. Tessa needs to sign a form, if she ever has a moment free. Someone *always* needs to sign a form! Bye, Helen. Lovely to run into you. Bye, Ben. Nice to meet you, too.'

'You haven't said much about Maddie,' Ben's mother went as they drove home. Ben gave yet another mumble.

TWENTY-FIVE

He did quite a lot of schoolwork that night, especially the work he should have done already. He thought of Mrs Sione's words: *Don't let yourself down . . . See it as a challenge.* Yeah, he promised himself again, he was gonna give things his best shot. Not just school: everything.

He thought of other words as well. Those ones from Maddie's mother kept replaying in his head. *Maddie's been telling me about you.* What had she said?

His stump felt sore. Not too bad, but tired and aching. All that standing and moving around on it, of course. But hey, he'd walked on his own two feet! Well, on his own one foot and that metal rod. What would it be like when he got the proper prosthesis? He was going to give that his best shot, too.

When he'd done his exercises and was getting ready for bed later, he checked his stump. It looked fine, not red or anything. As he gazed, a weird feeling swept over him. He felt so *fond* of that stump. It had gone through something awful, put up with so much. I'll look after you, he promised — silently. I'll give you my very, *very* best shot.

He took his crutches to school on Tuesday. 'You've done brilliantly, son,' his father said, as he held the car door open in the parking lot and passed the crutches over. 'We're proud of you. Just stay careful, eh?'

And Ben was. (*Hell*, he thought; *I'm doing what my parents told me!*) He moved slowly through doorways; checked where he was landing the crutches' rubber tips on the ground; made sure he kept his steps — his hops — short. But oh man, it felt so good, looking people in the eye again.

He was the first to answer one of Mrs Sione's questions about their homework. She gave him a nod, and what Ben felt sure was a secret smile. At lunchtime, he watched his mates play soccer. Would he ever be able to do anything like that again? He felt himself sag a bit inside.

He watched Manu swerve past a tackler, send a perfect pass skimming forward. *That's my best mate*, he suddenly thought. *I hope he gets to play for a pro team.*

Then the ball came bouncing towards him, hit his right leg and stopped. The other guys watched uncertainly. Ben raised one crutch, and whacked the ball back onto the field, while people laughed and cheered.

At the end of the afternoon, he told Mrs Sione he'd be away on Wednesday morning. 'They're starting to fit the new leg.'

His teacher nodded again. 'I was wondering if you might like to talk to the form class about it, some time? Tell them about the accident, what things were like afterwards, how you've recovered so much. Because you have: we can all see that. Think about it, anyway.'

Ben did. Him talking to his class? No way. Though maybe . . .

Hom arrived soon after he got home. She checked his stump. 'Looking good. Remember to keep massaging with that olive oil and Vitamin E. We want the skin to be really healthy and supple for the prosthesis.'

Ben told her about the sudden tearing pain he'd had,

and his physio nodded. 'It will happen. You know what it is. If you can, do some massage and pinching straight after. It reminds your brain what is real.'

Ben grinned. 'How about if I'm out at Burger Land or somewhere there are heaps of people?'

Hom grinned back. 'You keep doing the pinching. It gives people things to talk about to their friends.'

She took him through his exercises; added still more weights to what he was lifting with his legs. 'You will need the strength when your prosthesis is on.'

'Have you seen Tim's eye?' Ben asked. Hom looked uncertain for a second; then she laughed. 'He is from a disaster movie.'

Then Ben asked her the question he'd been secretly preparing. 'Do you do any physio for people who've lost hands or arms?'

'Yes. There is one person.' Hom paused, and gave Ben a knowing look. 'I am not meant to give names. Are you thinking of someone we know?'

Ben shook his head; knew that his face was getting warm. 'Nah. I mean, I was just wondering.'

The physio smiled. 'I remember one patient, they had no hand since being born. Once, they tripped over, put their hand out to save themselves and their prosthetic hand was pushed into the stump. They needed massage and healing for that. Also a hand has to take stress — keyboarding, being hit by ball in sport, even cleaning teeth. We all need healthy skin and muscles, too. Just like you do, Ben. So — more exercises!'

'You are such a bully!' Ben groaned, and Hom laughed. He thought of the patient falling and ramming their prosthesis into the stump like that. Ouch. He thought of a name. Maddie Yelich.

Before dinner on Tuesday night, Ben's father handed him another banknote. 'Sold a couch, thanks to you. Elderly bloke with crook knees came in. So I pointed him at the one you said was easiest to get out of, and he liked it straightaway. Here's your sales commission. Have to get you to do some more testing. You up for that?'

'Yeah, sure,' Ben said. *I'm pulling in some serious money! Bet Manu and Connor haven't done this!*

On Wednesday morning, while his mother was driving his dad to work, Ben hung out the washing. His mum had just dropped things from the washing machine into the basket when Mr Coles called to her. 'Oh,' she exclaimed, 'I'll have to do this later. Can you be ready when I get home, Ben, love?'

So Ben waited till the car whirred off down the drive. Then he bent carefully, held on to the wall, and lifted the basket of washing under his other arm. With a single crutch, he hopped slowly, checking his balance at every step, ready to drop the basket if he began to topple, out to the clothesline, and placed it on the trolley. One piece at a time, crutch still tucked under his left elbow, he pegged the washing out, uneven but OK.

He'd just hopped back inside with the basket when his mother came hurrying through the front door. 'Ready, darling? I'll just hang out this —' She stopped, stared at the empty basket, stared at her grinning son, went 'Oh, Ben!', and threw her arms around him so hard he was almost knocked off his crutches.

Nobody else in the waiting room. Had Maddie finished getting her new prosthesis fixed up? Would she be at the hospital again? And why was he wondering about these things?

Tim appeared. His swollen eye had partly gone down but was now a vivid purple and yellow. Ben saw his mother staring, and went, 'It wasn't me, Mum.' Mrs Coles and Tim laughed. Prosthetist introduced himself to parent.

Parent introduced herself to prosthetist, then told Ben she had to drop into the polytech, but she'd be back in an hour. The other two headed down the corridor.

Inside the now familiar room with its wall bars and steps, Ben stopped dead. The equally familiar socket lay on the table. But it wasn't attached to the steel rod. Instead, it formed the top part of an amazingly, almost totally realistic-looking lower leg and foot.

TWENTY-SIX

'Metal rod's still in there,' Tim told him. 'Fibreglass and thermo-plastic shell around that. Looks like the real thing, eh? Foot's the most special part. Carbon graphite — there'll be a test on all this later, by the way.' He laughed as he saw Ben's face. 'Nah, just kidding. The foot's got two joints in it, for up and down, plus sideways movement. Whaddaya reckon?'

'It's awesome!' Ben exclaimed. 'Can I try it?'

The prosthetist laughed again. 'That's what you're here for, buddy. But we'll take our time, eh? We want to get things spot on with this, too.'

Ben sat down on the stool and Tim passed him the new leg. 'Hold it. Get used to the feel of it. There's some labs overseas trying to make prostheses with 3D printers, but till that happens properly, you're looking at a few thousand bucks' worth in there. So don't go using it to hammer in nails.'

Ben took the plastic shape. 'It's a lot heavier than just the rod.'

'Nearly all in the foot. And that means a couple of things. You'll need to learn balancing all over again. Your right side weighed more, up till now, with your own leg gone. Now it's almost the other way round. Artificial leg isn't actually heavier than a real one, but it'll feel that way for a while.'

Ben nodded and Tim went on, 'Plus from now on, you'll have this weight pulling on the socket and on your residual limb all the time. Not just when you're walking — when you're standing and sitting, even. So the socket gets wear and tear. That's natural. Can mean it fits less well after a while, but we'll keep checking for that.'

He took the leg from Ben. 'And remember you're still growing. We'll need to take it back from time to time; make the socket bigger, rod and foot longer.' Ben thought of Maddie and her new hands. He nodded again.

'All right, then. So here's the moment we've all been waiting for. You wanna do a drumroll?' He sat in front of Ben. 'Let's get this on and start you trying it out.' He checked the sock on Ben's stump. 'Some people give their prosthesis a name. You can think about that.'

Ben realised his heart was beating faster as Tim slipped the socket with its new leg and foot onto his stump and rolled the elastic bandage up over his knee. 'Try and work your residual limb around in there a few times. See if it's still feeling all right.'

Ben did. 'It's good. Tight, but not too tight.'

'OK. Now lift it up off the stool. Like you did when it was just the rod. It's heavier now, remember, so don't worry if you can't manage first time.'

Ben stared down at the creamy-coloured leg and foot stretching in front of him. He could see the joints where his new shin met his new ankle; could glimpse bits of metal, little levers and wheel shapes, inside. For a second, he felt panic that it would be like in the hospital that time; that his body wouldn't manage what his brain told it. But next moment, his left leg was rising steadily off the stool. It was heavier than before, all right, but he was doing it. He was doing it!

'Good,' Tim told him. 'Now down slowly. Don't let it flop. You gotta look after this thing, remember.'

Three more liftings and lowerings. Ben could feel the effort from his knee and thigh muscles.

The prosthetist stood. 'Now let's get you on your feet. OK to try without crutches? I'll hold you.'

'Sure.' Ben shifted his new limb off the stool, placed its foot on the floor. He stared at it for a moment, trying to believe what was happening. Tim counted 'One . . . two . . . three . . . up', and with the helping hand under one elbow, Ben rose to his feet.

Yes, his feet. Two of them. He wobbled a fraction, steadied, gazed down at the new prosthesis. It looked so solid. It *felt* solid and stable, too. He wasn't balancing on a small tip the way he'd been doing; his weight was spread over a wider area. Amazing. Brilliant!

A voice was speaking in his ear. 'You listening?' Tim went. 'I said you can stop grinning now.'

But the shaven-headed figure was smiling, too, as he let go of Ben's elbow and moved to stand in front of him. 'Can you stay like that for a bit, buddy? Try and keep as even as possible. I want to see if you look balanced. Grab the wall bar the moment you get wobbly.'

He moved slowly around Ben. 'Looks like you might be a millimetre or so high on the prosthesis side. Feel any difference there?'

'Not really,' Ben said. 'Seems good to me.'

A snort. 'That's 'cos you want it to be. Stay like that

another minute, if you can.' From the bench, Tim took his tape measure, ran it down Ben's right side from hip to ground, then did the same on the left side. 'Yeah, might shave a fraction off the heel there. That should fix it.'

'Can you do that now?' asked Ben. 'I can wear the leg home — can't I?'

'Sorry, mate. Don't want you doing too much on it till we've got it as near perfect as poss. Next time, with any luck. Now let's get you over to these bars.' He put his hand under Ben's elbow again; helped him take three steps to the pair of parallel bars that stretched at waist height across one side of the room.

'I want you to walk up and down between these a couple of times. Hold the bars to start with. Anything doesn't feel right, especially on the stump, you stop straightaway.' As Ben positioned himself between the bars, his prosthetist went on. 'Another thing about the foot: it's got limited plantar flexion.' Ben looked blank. Tim grinned again. 'Means it doesn't move up and down as easy as a real one. Real foot's got twenty-six bones and about a hundred muscles in it. It's moving and flexing all the time you're walking, though you hardly ever notice. This one's got its two joints, but they can only do a few up-and-down and sideways movements. Can mean a bit of a problem with the accelerator and brake when you buy your Maserati. Anyway, let's walk before you drive, so take it slowly.'

Hands on bars, Ben moved forward. Yeah, the left foot lifted slower than his other one. It took maybe a quarter-second longer for the toes to come down after its heel touched the ground. But by the time he'd walked between the bars five times, he was moving steadily. On the last lap, he lifted his hands off. Tim began to speak; went silent.

'Top stuff,' he said when Ben had finished. 'And that's enough for today. Let's have another look at your stump after all that.' Ben sat, the leg was removed, elastic bandage and sock rolled back. 'Looking good. See you Friday, OK? No promises — you'll need time, remember — but might be able to let you have the leg for this weekend, if you behave yourself.'

'Thanks, Tim. Thanks heaps.' As Ben was fitting the crutches under his elbows, he asked, 'You always done this job? Worked with artificial legs and stuff?'

The shaven head shook. 'Nah. Trained as a diesel mechanic. Worked for a forestry company our family ran. Helped look after their trucks and bulldozers. Then a cuzzie of me and Jake had a tree fall on him. Crushed his leg so bad, they had to amputate it. Jake was already working in the hospital, kept me up to speed with what was happening to Rawiri. So I got interested; did some courses, learned a whole lot of stuff. Now here I am.'

'Cool,' went Ben, then felt silly at what he'd said. 'Your cousin — Rawiri? — sounds a bit like what happened to me.'

Tim was placing the leg back on his bench. 'Yeah, except his had to be a transfemoral amputation — just below the hip. Takes a long time to recover from that: big arteries and bones and muscles to look after. Prosthesis needs a knee joint as well as an ankle one. Tricky stuff.'

'He all right now?' Ben asked.

'Back with the forestry gang, would you believe?' Tim half-laughed. 'Cheeky sod. Sometimes he goes into a shop, leaves his dirty boots at the door like they ask you to, leaves his leg standing in its boot as well. Scares the hell out of other customers. OK, buddy, we'll see you on Friday.'

Ben was smiling as he and his crutches made their way back along the corridor. Not just at Tim's story, but at how great it had felt walking on two legs and two feet. He couldn't wait till Friday. Yes, he could. He *would*. And he'd be sensible; take things carefully.

The waiting room was still empty, he saw, as he approached the doorway. He swung himself inside and realised he was wrong. Maddie Yelich was sitting there and watching him.

TWENTY-SEVEN

The first thing Ben noticed was her hand. She wasn't wearing the red mitten today; maybe she'd got used to the new prosthesis. It was the same creamy colour as his own new leg and foot. The same sort of elastic bandage too, reaching from her wrist onto her forearm. The fingers were curved; he glimpsed little slits where they met the palm. Joints, he guessed, also like his foot. All those things he'd never have noticed before.

He knew he was staring at it; began to turn away, then stopped. 'Looks good.'

Maddie glanced down. 'Feels good, too. Tessa's still checking and checking it. They're so fussy.'

'Fair enough.' He was thinking, *Still checking: that means she'll be coming in for a while yet.*

He blinked as Maddie laughed suddenly. 'It's much stronger than the old one. I picked up a glass yesterday to dry, and it broke while I was holding it.'

Ben winced. 'You cut yourself?' Then he realised. 'Aw, duh!'

They both laughed. 'What's happening with yours? Your new leg?' she asked. So he told her how he'd had it on for the first time just now, had stood and walked on it — in it — and how it felt so brilliant.

She was smiling. 'Cool.' Ben nodded. 'Yeah, cool.'

They both went silent. Ben tried to think of something — anything — to say. 'You seen Angus?'

Maddie shook her head. 'Not since last week. He's got some health issues, I think. Never complains, though.'

More silence, then she spoke again. 'My mum says your mum's really nice.'

Ben felt surprised. Yeah, she was, but she was just his mum, like his dad was . . . well, just his dad. 'Hey, meant to tell you —' (he hadn't, but the words were suddenly there) '— Mrs Sione, my English teacher at school, she wants me to talk to our class about what . . . what happened to me. Have you —?'

Maddie was already nodding. 'When I was at primary school, I had to talk to the whole school assembly! There were three of us: Samuel, he's this blind guy; and Josefina who's got cerebral palsy so she's, like, in a wheelchair all the time; and me. I looked at the other two and I thought, who wants to hear about me and my hand after listening to Sam and Josie?'

I want to hear about you, Ben thought, yet he half-understood. 'What *did* you talk about?'

'Oh, I —' But someone else was entering the room. Ben's mother.

'Hi, love. Sorry if I kept you waiting.' She looked at the girl. 'You're Maddie? Hello.' She nodded towards Ben. 'I'm this creature's mother.'

Maddie laughed; shot a quick look at Ben. He began levering himself up on his crutches. 'How did it go, love?' Mrs Coles was asking.

'OK,' Ben said. 'See you,' he told the girl. She nodded, went 'See you' back. *She didn't say what she gave her talk about*, he thought, as he and his mother left. *Next time, maybe . . .* whatever he meant by that.

School on Wednesday afternoon was boring, and Ben felt glad. Boring meant things were getting back to normal (that danger word again). Every day, fewer kids took any notice of him on his crutches. One guy even let a corridor door swing shut in Ben's face, and Manu had to grab the handle. 'Watch it, bro!' he called after the boy, who went, 'What's your prob—', saw Ben, and gulped, 'Aw, sorry.' Girls who'd fussed over him before just said 'Hi', and kept going. 'Looks like the super-hot guy's cooling down,' sniggered Connor, and Ben thumped him with a crutch.

His stump felt sore by the time he got home. His neck and back ached. The short walk on his prosthesis at the hospital had been harder on his body than he realised. But he kept thinking how great being on two feet had felt. Roll on, Friday!

He was doing some homework before tea when he bent to scratch an itch in his leg. He realised it was his left leg and stopped. The itch kept on; grew more annoying. He unpinned the flap of his jeans, began taking off the sock that covered his stump.

His dad, who'd come into the living room, looked concerned. 'You OK, mate? You need —?' Ben shook his head. 'I'm all right.' He massaged the stump; pinched all around it. But the itch remained; didn't fade until dinner time. It was worse than a pain; he snapped at his mother when she asked about it. Just when he thought everything was coming right, turned out it wasn't.

At school on his crutches the next day (roll on *faster*, Friday!), Ben told Mrs Sione that yeah, he'd give a talk to the form class. 'Excellent!' his teacher smiled. 'Next week, maybe? We'll sort it out.'

He went to the library at lunchtime. His mates were out playing soccer again. He'd like to be there, even just watching, but they needed a bit of time off from looking after him. And . . . well, soccer wasn't for him anymore. He had to face up to that. *Hope Manu keeps playing*, he thought again.

His mother had just parked their car in the drive after school when Hom arrived. The physio watched Ben work his way up the ramp on his crutches. 'Perhaps the steps will be easier with the new leg. You can ask tomorrow.'

'So Tim told you I'm getting it if I've behaved myself?' Ben asked.

His physio seemed to blush a little. 'It is part of my job to know. Now —' she spoke briskly '— we check your stump; make sure it is perfect for when the leg comes on. The hygiene is so important. You are washing it carefully in the shower?'

Ben nodded. Yeah, he had been — when he

remembered. Hom ran her tape measure around his stump. 'No sign of fluid. Very good. The prosthesis may not need many changes. Tim will watch. So will I. Right, we do the exercises.'

They did. *Wonder if I'll ever be able to stop the bum-squeezing?* Ben thought. 'Those weights you got me to lift were really useful,' he told Hom. 'The prosthesis is quite heavy, but I'm managing fine.

'Oh,' he went on. 'I had this major itch yesterday. Really annoying.'

Hom nodded. 'You know what to do. Was it a burning feeling, too?' When Ben shook his head, she said, 'Good. A burning sometimes means infection.' She began packing up her gear. 'Two hundred years ago, there was no anaesthetic for surgeries. Strong people held the patient down, put a piece of wood in the mouth to bite on for the pain, while the surgeon worked as fast as possible. It would take just ten minutes to amputate a leg. Often the instruments were dirty. The wound became infected, and the patient died.'

She smiled at Ben. 'Now an amputation like yours takes five . . . six hours. Everything is clean — sterile. The patient sleeps like a baby and feels nothing.'

Ben nodded. He felt . . . well, he felt glad he hadn't been tramping on Pangonui two hundred years ago.

TWENTY-EIGHT

'Interested in another couple of hours' work tomorrow?' Mr Coles asked at breakfast on Friday. Yes, Ben was interested. Definitely interested: he was making some good coin here. 'A bit different from last time,' his dad told him. 'You'll be —'

His mum's phone rang. 'Yes? Speaking. Oh, hello. Yes, he's here; I'll pass you over.' She handed the phone to Ben. 'Tim. From the hospital.'

Aw, no, they weren't going to cancel, were they? He'd been counting the hours till he could get his new leg. 'Hello?' he went.

'Kia ora, mate. Tim from Prosthetics here. Listen, when you come in this morning, can you bring your other shoe? Your left one? Forgot to ask you on Wednesday.'

'My other . . .?' Ben understood. 'Yeah, sure.'

'Everything OK?' his father wanted to know. Ben explained. 'He must want to try it on the prosthesis.'

His mother smiled. 'You're doing so well, darling. I'll drop your dad at work, then I'll be back for you. Better see if you can find your other shoe.'

It was in the bottom of his wardrobe. An ordinary white sneaker with black stripes, a bit dusty and somehow lost-looking. Ben gazed at it. Last time he'd had this on, four . . . nearly five weeks ago, everything had been ordinary, sometimes boring. OK, he had to admit that his life since then had hardly ever been boring.

He did the breakfast dishes — washed them, dried them, put them away, leaning against the sink and bench to keep his balance. This time tomorrow, he could be standing on two legs to do it.

His prosthesis lay on Tim's table. Ben passed his left sneaker over to the prosthetist, who slipped it onto the artificial foot and tied the laces. He lifted the leg and shook it. The sneaker stayed firm. 'Good. Fits OK.' He passed the leg to Ben, who felt the weight again as he cradled it in his hands.

'Right, you put it on,' The shaven-headed tech told him. 'You gotta get used to that. Try to do it the same way each time, if you can. Makes it easier on the stump and socket.'

Ben eased his half-leg into the snug bowl of the socket, rolled the elastic sleeve into position over his knee. 'Up when you're ready,' went Tim, and with a helping hand under his elbow, Ben worked himself up onto his feet. The leg already felt familiar; still felt brilliant.

'OK, now you use this for a while.' The prosthetist lifted something else from the table. A walking stick.

Ben stared. 'I don't need —'

Tim shook his head. 'Yeah, yeah, I know you don't want to look like an old guy. But right now, the leg and your stump matter most. I've seen too many people have a fall or something, stuff up the prosthesis, hurt themselves. Plus you've got to get used to moving around in crowds, and the stick sends people a signal; tells them to let you have a bit of room.'

Once more, Tim measured both legs from hip to ground, then stepped back, gazing at Ben as he stood.

'Do I really need this?' Ben pointed at the walking stick. 'I can manage. I did on Wednesday.'

'You had the bars to help you then.' Tim glanced at him. 'OK. Walk forward four steps, then turn right and walk four more. I'll be there to grab you if anything happens.'

It won't, Ben told himself. Standing on two feet only, he moved forward. Right foot. Left foot, lifting the prosthesis, taking a small step only, putting it down. A tiny wobble, but fine. Right foot again. Left foot carefully. No probs. He didn't need a stick.

'Now turn right.' Tim was close beside him.

Easy. Ben swivelled on his own leg, and swung the prosthesis around. Its weight took it further than he meant to. Much further. As it came down, he lurched, flung his arms sideways, began toppling over. Instantly, Tim had him, holding him up. 'See what I mean? You need that stick at first. You've got the ramp at home, Hom tells me.' Tim seemed to hesitate a second. 'And there'll be steps in places you haven't noticed. So use it till you're really sure.'

Ben realised he was shaking. He'd so nearly done a face plant, like that time on the back path. 'Yeah. OK.'

'This is your first prosthesis,' Tim told Ben as he passed him the walking stick. 'Like I said, we'll be making you others as you grow up. We do lifelong care, buddy. Another fifty years, and you could end up with one of my grandkids looking after you. Scary, eh?'

Ben grinned. When he tried to imagine one of Tim's grandkids, he saw a little guy with a shaven head.

With the prosthetist close by, he walked carefully around the room. Right turns were still tricky, but he was learning to allow for the extra weight of his new leg. And ordinary walking felt so brilliant. As he did his fourth or fifth lap, Tim stood in front, watching him approach. 'Good. Putting a shoe on sometimes nudges the foot offline, but yours seems OK. Now let's try the hard part.'

The hard part was steps: one of the sets positioned around the room, with handrails on both sides. 'Going up's easier, so we'll do that first. Lift your left knee higher than you usually would. Lean forward while you step up. One hand on the rail, one hand on your stick. Or both hands on the rails. Don't be afraid to ask someone to carry the stick, eh? People like doing good deeds.'

Ben managed with the stick plus one hand, and felt pleased. He managed going down the steps as well, though that was harder.

'Lean back a bit, like with the crutches,' Tim told him. 'Stick and prosthesis forward together — make sure they're both down before you bring the right leg through. It's another thing you've done millions of times before, but never had to think about.'

'Can I keep wearing it? Can I use it at school?' Ben asked, when he'd gone up and down the steps four times.

'Hmmm.' Tim grunted. 'How's the stump feeling?'

'It's fine. Really comfortable.'

'OK, then. But take your crutches along as well. No, *listen!* I know how much you want to walk in there on your own feet. But like I've been telling you, we need to look after that stump. If it starts to feel the slightest bit sore, you take off the leg and start using the crutches. Get the pressure off your residual leg. Deal?'

Ben nodded. 'One more thing,' Tim went on. 'Wash the prosthesis every day. Soap and warm water. Keep it clean like you keep your stump clean. And don't expect your mother to do it. Second deal?'

They were both grinning. 'All right, buddy,' said the prosthetist. 'Have a great weekend. I'll see you Monday. On your way, then. You'll be wanting to get to school and learn something.'

'Thanks, Tim.' Ben kept grinning as he walked slowly, carefully, the few metres to the waiting room. He could hear his mother talking. He heard another voice as well: Mrs Yelich.

He came through the doorway, leaning slightly on his stick, knowing that a huge stupid smile was stretched across his face. Maddie's mother saw him first; exclaimed, 'Look at you!' His own mum's head whipped around. She stared at him for a second, then her hands flew up to her cheeks, and she began crying.

TWENTY-NINE

Thank hell there's nobody else here, thought Ben over the next couple of minutes. His mother jumped up, rushed over and threw her arms around him, nearly knocking the walking stick from his hand. 'Oh, Ben! You — you —' Then she started crying again. Mrs Yelich handed her a couple of tissues. Tim, who'd appeared with Ben's crutches, grinned, said, 'Happens nearly every time. He's doing fine,' and went away.

Finally, Ben and his mother sat down, while Maddie's mum passed over another tissue. 'Aren't they just amazing here? They've been so wonderful with us.'

Ben's mum, who still hadn't let go of him, squeezed his hand, gasped, 'I'm probably not safe to drive. I'll go and wash my face. Oh, son!' She stared at his prosthetic leg, neatly side by side with his own one as he sat, shook her head, and hurried out of the room.

'I was the same when Maddie got her first hand.' Mrs Yelich smiled at Ben. She really looked like her daughter, Ben realised. Same fair hair, same no-nonsense look. 'She was just a toddler, and the hand seemed such a tiny thing. She used to go around pretending she was a robot and scaring her friends at Playcentre.' Ben remembered Maddie telling him how her new prosthesis had accidentally shattered a glass.

'She tells me you're giving a talk to your school,' Mrs Yelich went on. 'That's great, Ben. People need to understand what it's like.'

'Yeah. It's to my form class, actually. Haven't decided what to say yet.' *Is she here?* Ben wondered meanwhile. *Must be in with Tessa. How long till she comes out? And she's . . . she's been saying more about me to her mother?*

Mrs Yelich was still talking, '. . . some ideas, if you want.' Ben blinked, tried to focus. 'Sorry?'

The girl's mother looked amused. 'I said Maddie can maybe give you some ideas on what to say, if you're interested. You want her number?'

'I . . . aw, yeah. Yeah, thanks.' He entered the digits in his own phone as Mrs Yelich read them out, hesitated, then put just *M.Y.* for the name.

'Like to give me yours?' The woman asked next. 'I'll pass them on.' Ben mumbled his number to her. *I can't just ring her up*, he was thinking. *And I won't know what to say if she calls me.* Too many things were happening again.

His mum reappeared. 'I hope you're ashamed of yourself, Ben Coles — making your mother behave like that. Let's get you off to school, where you're someone else's problem. Bye, Bridget. Best to Maddie.'

'Bye, Helen. Bye, Ben.' The other woman smiled. Ben gave yet another mumble. His mother picked up his crutches, and he set off slowly along the corridor. 'Be careful, won't you, darling,' his mum was saying. 'I know you're so thrilled, but make sure —'

'— make sure you don't rush, Mum,' Ben grinned. His mother pretended to swat him on the head. People coming towards them stared or smiled.

A guy from his form class was crossing the school carpark as Mrs Coles drove in. 'Hey, Api, could you carry these for me?' Ben called. He pulled his crutches from the back seat, holding on to the door handle as he did so. 'Bye, Mum. Make sure you don't rush in the traffic,' he said. His mother poked her tongue out at him and drove off.

He set off towards his classroom, Api walking beside him, staring at the prosthesis and going, 'That's amazing. Is it hard to use?' No, it wasn't, provided he stepped carefully and allowed for the new weight. The toe of his left sneaker half-caught on the ground a couple of times; maybe he'd better tell Tim about that. He wobbled ever so slightly as they moved from carpark tarseal onto grass. OK, Tim was right about the walking stick; he did need it.

The class glanced up as he came in. When they saw Ben was walking on two legs, they began standing, going 'Hey, awesome!' . . . 'It's Optimus Prime!' . . . 'Look at that!' Api parked the crutches against the back wall. Up the front, Mrs Sione laughed and called, 'All right. English lesson on pause. Can you come up here, Ben, so we can embarrass you?'

He moved slowly between the desks. A narrow aisle like this was harder; his balance felt shaky, and his walking stick kept whacking against the furniture. But he made it. Mrs Sione pushed her chair forward, and he lowered himself down. *Hey*, he thought, *I'm a teacher!*

For five minutes, kids asked questions. 'How does it stay on? What's it made of? Do you get to keep it? Can it walk by itself?' (The last one was from Connor — of course.) Then Mrs Sione went, 'Right, that's enough for now. Ben can tell you more when he gives his talk . . . next Tuesday all right for you, Ben?'

He gulped and nodded.

It had begun to rain, so he stayed in his form room at lunchtime and talked to his mates. 'Send your leg off to the cafe, eh? Tell it to bring us some doughnuts,' said Connor — again, of course.

Prosthesis and residual leg felt good, though his stump was starting to ache. But each time he glanced down at his two legs side by side under the desk, his two feet firmly on the floor, it looked so brilliant.

The bell rang for end of lessons, and Mr Tran their Maths teacher wished them a good, safe weekend. Miriana, at the desk next to Ben's, jumped up. 'Gotta hurry, guys! Going to Auntie Ripeka's!' She pushed her way into the aisle, caught her bag on a chair, stumbled and half-fell against Ben's desk, shoving it sideways. She looked down, then stared at him. 'I'm so sorry! You all right? Did I hurt you?'

Ben stared back. 'Why?'

'I trod on your foot. Your . . . your new one. Sorry. Does it hurt?'

Ben peered down. There on top of his sneaker was the mark of a shoe. A shoe Miriana's size. He looked at the carbon fibre and plastic shape inside his sneaker, looked at Miriana, and grinned. 'Didn't feel a thing. Did *it* hurt *you*?'

He caught the toe of his left sneaker on the ground again as he made his way to the carpark, Manu carrying the crutches. Yeah, he'd better tell Tim about that. And his stump was definitely aching. He massaged around it while his mum drove home. She glanced down. 'Sore, love?' Ben nodded. 'A bit. I'll take the leg off and check it when I get home.'

The stump looked fine; just slightly pink in a couple of places. He began to fit the leg back on, remembered what Mr Dev and Tim and Hom and his mum and dad and half the planet had told him about not rushing things, and left it off. He texted Connor and Manu, arranged to meet sometime on Saturday, ate with his parents, carried dishes to the sink, hopping the three steps between table and bench while his mum watched but said nothing. He sat on his bed; started a game of *Exploding Kittens* on his laptop, realised his back, shoulders, neck and hips ached as well. He propped the prosthesis in a corner of his room, where it wouldn't fall, and where he could see it, and slept like he was lying at the bottom of the sea.

In the middle of the night he woke, and it took him a moment to remember things. When he did, a sadness he hadn't expected began creeping into him. Why was he getting so excited about an artificial leg? OK, he'd come a long way, like people said. But he'd give everything — *everything* — to be back on Pangonui before the accident, so he could somehow stop all of this from happening.

THIRTY

'You and your designer leg want to come to the shop this morning?' Mr Coles asked with a grin at breakfast. 'Got something else you could help us with.'

'Yeah, sure. Oh, hey — I'm supposed to wash my leg every day. I forgot last night; can I do it before I go?'

'I don't think it'll be ready in time,' his mother told him.

'Doesn't matter. It'll dry off while I wear it.'

'It's got that mesh inside the socket, son,' his dad said. 'That'll take a while to dry. Should you be wearing it while that's still damp? What did Tim —'

'It'll be OK!' Ben interrupted him.

'How about you leave washing it till we get home?' said his mother, after a moment's silence. 'Maybe start doing it before you go to bed? That'll give it time to dry.'

Ben knew she was right. His father was right, too, about not trying to wash and wear it now. So he grunted.

He made his way slowly down the ramp to where his dad waited by the car. If he leaned back, like he'd practised on those steps with Tim, and braced himself on the walking stick before he moved his right leg through, that made things easier. His father watched; Ben could tell he was ready to leap forward if anything went wrong.

'Well done, Ben!' a voice called when he reached the path. He saw Mrs Bhatiani on the footpath. 'You should see him doing his tight-rope routine,' Mr Coles called back to her.

'All set for another superb selling session?' his father asked, as they reached The Great Indoors.

'No problem,' Ben said. And it wasn't. He was able to hold on to the double beds that two elderly couples were thinking about, move around, and tuck in the demonstration duvet. One old lady told him he was 'an impressive young man'. His father said he'd earned another pay packet, and passed it over. That was all good.

Back home, he washed the prosthetic leg in the laundry

tub with fabric softener, rinsed it, stood it upside-down in the back porch to dry. 'How about we hang it on the line?' he asked his mother. She snorted. 'I'll hang *you* on the line!' That was all gooder.

So when Connor and Manu walked round later (*someday I'll walk to* their *places*, Ben promised himself), he told his mother that they'd head to Burger Land and spend some of his earnings. He'd leave the leg behind, use his crutches, be extra careful, sit and rest there. 'Anyway, if I get too sore these guys can carry me part of the way. They need to get fit.' So Manu and Connor pretended to be insulted, and that was goodest of all.

The three of them made it to Burger Land, sat and ate and laughed and cracked jokes about one another. Connor cracked most of the jokes, of course. Some kids from school came in, went 'Looking good, Ben'. He covered the couple of blocks back home OK on his crutches. People who saw him coming along the footpath gave him plenty of room.

His back ached. Funny how ordinary things like walking — things that used to be ordinary, anyway — used muscles you never thought of.

On Sunday, he did some schoolwork; tried to decide what he was going to say to the form class; couldn't decide; looked at Maddie Yelich's number on his phone; couldn't decide about that, either. But he still felt good. Good enough to give Millie and Margie another ride in the wheelchair when they, plus Aunt Josie and Uncle Kyle, dropped in later. He walked carefully behind the twins in his prosthesis, announced he was going to tip them into the gutter, and they squealed again.

'Hurting at all?' Tim asked on Monday, after Ben walked proudly with his stick into the prosthetist's room.

'Not really. Back gets a bit sore, though.'

Tim checked the stump, looked inside the socket, running his finger slowly over its surfaces, and nodded. 'You gotta keep doing your exercises, remember. All your muscles are having to work harder to move you around with that leg.'

He got Ben to walk over to one set of parallel bars. A wooden block stood between them. 'New exercise today. Want you to move your right leg up onto that block; hold it a second; bring it down again. We call it "tap-ups". Means your weight keeps going on the prosthesis. OK?'

'That all?' Ben asked. 'Just move my right leg up and down?'

'You'll see,' The prosthetist told him. 'Hold the bars — yeah, even if you think you don't need to. Twelve times. Go.'

The first four were easy. The next four, Ben could feel the weight coming onto his stump and the prosthesis; knew he was starting to wobble. The last four, he was grunting with effort. He would have toppled sideways if he hadn't been holding the bars.

'I want you doing that at home, too,' Tim said, when Ben had finished and stood panting. 'Use a couple of books for the step. Make sure you've got something to hold on to. OK, now let's do it the other way round. Stand on your right leg; tap-ups with the new foot. Go.'

This was easier. A couple of times, the new leg took a quarter-second to respond. Once, its sneaker almost snagged on the edge of the step. But his own right leg stood steady.

'That left foot catching sometimes?' Tim asked, at the end. 'I can shorten the prosthesis, shave a bit off the sneaker toe. I'll need to have the leg till Friday.'

Ben hesitated. Four days on crutches again. Four days looking like an old man at school. 'Nah,' he lied. 'It's not a problem.'

Tim was looking hard at the new leg and foot. 'We want to get this really right, remember? Any issues, best we deal with them now.'

Ben shook his head. 'I'll be fine.'

'OK, then. Now — you got any tight jeans?' As Ben looked puzzled, Tim went on. 'Prosthesis is bulkier than your own leg; you've probably noticed that. Tight jeans can be a pain to get on and off.'

Ben shrugged. 'My pants are just . . . ordinary size.'

'That's cool. Those stressed jeans, the ones with rips in them, they're a problem. Prosthesis catches on the torn bits; tears them even bigger. All right, then, buddy, if you're feeling good, we'll leave it till Friday for the next appointment. Tell your . . . Tell Hom if things get sore at all. You're doing great. Just keep taking it easy. Don't —'

'— Don't go rushing off up a mountain,' Ben interrupted, and smirked. 'I won't. Thanks, Tim.'

He set off down the corridor and into the waiting room. 'Well, well,' a voice said. 'Who's this fit-looking laddie?'

Angus sat smiling at him. A couple of seats away, another person watched him as well. 'Maddie here was telling me ye had the new leg. That's great news, son. How's it feeling?'

'Good. Really good.' And it was, especially now these

two had seen him moving on it. *I was meant to contact her*, Ben was thinking meanwhile. *Will she be in a mood because I didn't?*

'Grand. Grand.' The old man smiled again. He was resting both hands on his walking stick, Ben saw, slightly hunched forward over it. 'And I hear you're going to be making a speech to your class about what happened. Good idea, laddie. Help them understand a wee bit more. People need —'

He stopped as Tim appeared. 'Morning, Angus. You've got to put up with me today.'

'A pleasure.' Angus heaved himself up, swayed for a second. Tim moved quickly towards him. 'You OK?'

The old man waved him away. 'Just overcome with the pleasure of seeing you, Tim, lad. Lead the way.' As they began leaving the room, Angus winked and said, 'I'm sure you two have lots to talk about — young Ben's speech, I mean.'

Then his face changed, seemed to go serious. He looked at boy and girl, went, 'Be kind — every time you can.'

'What's he on about?' Ben asked, when Angus and Tim had gone.

The girl shook her head. 'Dunno. He's been . . .' She turned to Ben. 'Hey, meant to ask you — what's it like going to a co-ed school?'

'Just ordinary,' Ben told her. 'What's it like going to an all-girls school?'

'Just ordinary,' Maddie told him. They both laughed, looked at each other, then looked at the ground. After a moment the girl asked, 'So, what are you going to say to your class?'

THIRTY-ONE

He was going to say what happened on the mountain, he told Maddie. How it was his fault for being in a hurry. How he was trapped under the boulder, and all he could think of was whether he'd smashed his teeth. The chopper ride, the first days in hospital, his mother crying when she told him about his leg. (Actually, he might leave out that part; it made him choke up, too.) The phantom pains, the wheelchair and crutches and exercises and prosthesis. *Man*, he thought, *I'll need two speeches*.

'You going to show them your leg?' Maddie asked.

'They've already seen it.'

'No, I mean take it off and let them see inside. When I did my talk, I took my hand off —' she lifted her right arm; no mitten on the prosthesis today; she was getting used to it, all right — 'and they were rapt. Most of them, anyway. I couldn't pass it round the whole assembly, but you can probably do it with just your class — if they're careful.'

'As long as my mates don't start trying to kick one another with it,' Ben said, and she laughed. 'When are you doing it?' she asked. 'The speech?'

'Tomorrow.' As the girl kept watching him, he went, 'I reckon I know what to say now. Good idea about passing the leg round. Thanks.'

A few seconds' silence, then Maddie went, 'Being up on the mountain. What's it like?'

'Brilliant!' Ben told her. 'You can see for ever. Seems like that, anyway. And there's the snow and the bush and those boulders and —'

Another voice spoke. 'Kia ora Maddie.' It was Tessa. 'Ready to come along?'

The girl stood. As she was leaving with the prosthetist, she turned like Angus had done. 'Good luck. Let's know how the talk goes. And — I'd like to hear more about the mountain, sometime.'

The talk went brilliantly. *So it should have*, Ben told himself afterwards. He'd spent nearly all of Monday after school and through the evening, writing it out and learning it. He'd stopped to have tea, then to wash his prosthesis and put it in the shower to dry. ('Have to warn anyone staying here,' Mr Coles grinned. 'Else they'll get a nasty shock when they pull the shower curtain back.')

Ben sat at the front of the class (in Mrs Sione's chair again; *I could get to like this*, he thought). He described the shingle slopes, the boulder toppling on him almost in slow motion, the rescue teams and his dad fighting to dig him out, being winched up to the chopper. He said how he hadn't understood for the first few days what had happened to him. He talked about all the people who had helped him — Mr Dev, Jake, the other nurses, Hom and Tim. 'And my mum and dad: they've been awesome.'

He paused, said, 'I feel down about it sometimes. There's things I know I'm never gonna be able to do again. But I'm giving it my best shot. And the best thing *you* can do is treat me just like any other guy.'

The class sat silent. A couple of times, Neve and Miriana and some other girls seemed to be dabbing at their cheeks. Now came the bit Maddie had suggested. 'OK, this is how it comes off,' he told the class. He peeled down the elastic bandage and eased his leg out of the socket. He heard a few gasps as some people saw his stump for the first time.

'It fits really tight and comfortably. The foot part can go up and down, and from side to side a bit. I'll pass it round. It's quite heavy, so don't drop it, eh?' He heard Tim's voice in his head. *There's a few thousand bucks' worth in there.*

A couple of kids screwed up their faces, and passed the prosthesis on without looking, but most ran their hands over it, touched the ankle joints, looked inside the socket. More questions came: 'Will it go rusty?' . . . 'Does it have batteries?' Someone wanted to know if scientists would ever be able to grow a new leg from stem cells. 'I'll be first in the queue if they do,' Ben said, and the class laughed.

When he finished, everyone clapped, and there were even a few whistles. Manu and Connor whistled loudest, of course. 'That was great, Ben,' Mrs Sione smiled.

'You aren't like any other guy, bro,' Manu told him at lunchtime. 'You're a bit special, eh?' Ben went 'Aw, crap!', but didn't mind.

Hom checked his stump that afternoon, and watched him do his tap-up exercises, with a couple of thick books on the ground and a chair on each side to hold on to. She got him to try picking things up from the floor, first on the right (easy), then on the left (not easy). His prosthesis meant he couldn't just bend and grasp. He had to half-kneel; allow for the new leg's weight pulling him forward or holding him back. 'More for you to practise,' his physio told him.

Then she and he tossed a small bean bag backwards and forwards between them. Gradually, Hom made him reach a little further each time to catch, and he realised his prosthesis was making little shifts, the foot moving sideways or forwards as his arms stretched out. Another thing he'd never realised his own leg had done. 'You practise this, too, please,' The physio told him. 'With someone who is a good catcher.'

That rules Mum out, Ben thought. He pretended to be exhausted. 'When am I going to sleep?' he asked Hom. But he felt good once more.

Wednesday. He hung out with his mates at lunchtime. 'Hey, can you make it to Burger Land after school?' Manu asked. 'My turn to shout. Uncle Matiu paid me and Miriana for helping set things up last week at the

Community Centre for some big meeting, so I'm a millionaire.'

'Miriana?' Ben asked, and Connor went, 'You holding out on us, bro?'

'No questions, no problems,' Manu told them. 'You OK to get there, Ben?'

Ben hesitated, then said, 'Like you say, no problems. Meet you there.'

His mother was waiting in the carpark after school. How long till he was able to make his own way home? When she asked what he had planned for the rest of the afternoon, he began to say something about going to Burger Land with the others, then went silent.

Anyway, there was another thing he had to do first. While his mother was in her office, Ben went to his bedroom, took out his phone, started scrolling through his contacts. He found *M.Y.*, glanced at his watch. Would she still be on her way home from school? He'd wait till . . . But his fingers were already tapping her number.

As it started ringing, he swallowed. *Let's know how it goes*, she'd said. *But what if she didn't really want to* . . . The ringing stopped, and her voice spoke. 'Hi. So how did the talk go?'

Ben was sure he heard a *thunk!* as his jaw dropped open. 'How — how — did you know it was me?'

'You gave Mum your number, remember? She forwarded it to me. So how was the talk?'

'Oh, OK. No, actually, it was good — I think. Hey, thanks for that idea of passing round the . . . the leg. That really worked.'

'Cool. Any of them *not* want to look at it?'

Ben's jaw made the same sound again. 'Yeah. How did you know that?'

Maddie laughed. 'Same with my hand. If I take it off, for swimming or anything, there's kids who go "Oh, yuck!"; don't want to see it or the stump. Pathetic, eh? Makes me want to stick one of its fingers up their nose.'

Now Ben laughed. 'Yeah, they're pathetic, all right. Anyway, thanks.' He tried to make his next words sound as casual as he could. 'You gonna be at the clinic on Friday?'

'Not sure. Tessa says the new hand's working OK now. Feels good. I haven't smashed any more glasses, anyway. So I probably won't need to come in, unless there's an issue.'

Ben wasn't sure what to say. 'OK,' he went after a second.

The girl was silent also. Then: 'If you see Angus, can you say hello from me. And . . . could you give me a text or a call about how he's looking? I think there's something wrong, though he doesn't talk about it. You saw what he was like on Monday?'

Ben remembered the old man hunched forward over his walking stick, the wobbling as he stood. 'Yeah. Sure, I'll let you know.'

'Thanks.' Another pause. 'See you.'

'See you.' Ben ended the call and sat staring at his bedroom wall. In fact, it sounded like he might not see her again. How did he feel about that?

Manu — he'd nearly forgotten his mate's invitation. Stick in hand, he walked through to where his mother had just emerged from her office. His stump had begun to ache in its prosthesis, but he ignored it. 'Mum, I'm going round to Burger Land. Manu and Connor want to meet me there.'

His mum looked at him. 'Oh, Ben! You won't want your dinner.'

'I'll be all right. I'll head off now.'

Mrs Coles frowned. 'You've been on your leg all day. Look — can you wait a couple of minutes? Then I'll drive you there. You know you shouldn't be trying to do too much. I wish you'd told me before.'

Ben could feel bad temper welling up inside him. Maddie saying she might not be at the clinic anymore; his stump feeling sore; now his mother nagging at him. 'I forgot, that's all! You don't need to drive me. I've got there before, and I can do it again!'

'Ben —'. But he was already moving into the hall, shoving the door back so it banged against the wall, heading for the ramp to the outside. He'd show his mother, and everyone else. He wrenched the back door open. His walking stick whacked against it, chipping off a flake of paint. He wanted to kick the stupid thing, as hard as he could.

He ignored the wooden ramp. Stick in one hand, reaching for the rail with his other, he started down the steps.

The toe of his left sneaker caught on the concrete rim. He lurched; began toppling forward. His free hand grabbed at the rail; missed. The walking stick clattered from his hand. His body twisted, and all the weight thrust down suddenly on his prosthesis. Its foot seemed to jam; his leg refused to bend. His hands flailed at the air as he fought to stay balanced. 'Mum!' he heard himself yell. Then he was crashing down from the steps onto the concrete path below.

THIRTY-TWO

He got a hand half under himself as he landed; felt the rough surface rip at it like before. Then his left side and shoulder rammed into the concrete. Prosthesis and left knee hit hard as well, and the new leg seemed to buckle sideways, tearing at his stump. Pain clawed through it. 'Aaagh!' he howled.

For a couple of seconds, it was like the mountain and that other fall again. He lay crumpled up; the skin of his hand burning. The prosthesis wouldn't move. He tried to straighten his left leg, and agony tore up it from calf to thigh. 'Aaagh!' What had he done? What awful thing had happened?

'Ben!' His mother was there, kneeling beside him, staring. 'Oh, darling! What's happened?'

'Help — help me up!' His breath hissed between clenched teeth. 'I need you to — lift me.' More pain clutched at his leg, seized his knee this time. 'Aaagh!'

His mother was staring at his prosthesis. 'No, stay there! The new leg — it's all twisted. And Ben, you're bleeding!'

He could feel it now. Wetness and heat in his stump. 'Can you get the pros— the leg off?' He panted as more pain pulsed through him. God, he'd been so stupid! He'd . . . how bad was the stump?

His mum began rolling the elastic sleeve down. He could see the fear on her face. 'It's stuck. I can't — here it comes.' He felt the prosthesis fall away; yelled again as it dragged at his flesh. He glimpsed the leg as his mother dropped it on the path: the foot seemed twisted; its joint gaped open.

'Ben,' Mrs Coles was telling him. 'Ben, we need to get you to the hospital. Something's happened to the stump. There's a lot of blood, and I can't see where it's coming from. I'll get the car. No — wait. Don't move. Oh, darling!'

She vanished inside; was back almost instantly, talking fast into her phone, a cushion and towel clutched to her. 'His leg is bleeding . . . A lot. I can't see if . . . Yes, just him and me.'

She let the phone fall, next to his broken prosthesis; lifted his head gently and slipped the cushion underneath it. 'I'm putting the towel around your leg for the bleeding. Ben, love, just hold on.' Then she was kneeling beside him, gripping both his hands. The pain bit at his stump and leg; he shuddered and grunted.

Three . . . four minutes, and he heard a siren in the distance. His mother stayed kneeling by him, staring towards his stump, eyes flicking back to his face.

Footsteps hurried up the path. 'What's happened?' Mrs Tully from next door. 'Oh!' Her hand flew up to her mouth. 'What can I do?'

'He fell on the steps. His leg is bleeding — the hurt one. The ambulance is coming.' Mrs Coles spoke in jagged bursts. She clutched Ben's hands harder.

The siren wailed, louder and nearer. Ben turned his head on the cushion. He could just see his stump. The towel around it was sodden with blood, that had already seeped onto the concrete underneath. He could hear himself still panting; groaned as more pain wrenched at his leg. He'd done something terrible to himself, torn the stump wide open. They'd have to cut more of his leg off. How much? The whole leg? No! Please — no!

And it was his fault. He knew it as he lay there, his mother murmuring, 'They're almost here, love. You'll be all right.' Mrs Tully had disappeared, but now she returned with a rug that she spread over him. He kept shuddering and shaking. 'I'll look after the house, Helen. You go with Ben.'

Yes, his fault. He'd rushed into things, like everyone had told him not to. He'd ruined all that Tim and Hom and Mr Dev had done for him. And his parents and mates. Just because he was in a foul mood.

Tyres swung into the driveway. The siren died to a low growl, then silence. Ben could see its light flashing from where he lay. Doors slammed, and two figures in green uniforms appeared: a man and a woman. They moved quickly to where he sprawled on the concrete, his mother crouching beside him.

The man glimpsed Ben's stump, the towel around it soaked with blood. His face went stiff with shock; then he saw the smashed prosthesis and seemed to understand. The woman squatted down beside Mrs Coles. 'He fell?' As Ben's mother nodded, thc ambulance woman asked, 'What's his name?' Ben's mum told her, and she said more loudly, 'Ben? Ben, can you hear me?'

Of course I can hear you, a corner of Ben's brain thought stupidly. *I didn't fall on my ear.* Out loud, he managed to grunt a 'Yes', then stopped, his face twisting as more pain tore through him.

The man was now down beside him as well, a little torch in his hand. 'Just going to take a look at your eyes, buddy.' *It's my leg that's . . .* the same bit of Ben's brain began, then understood. A light shone in one eye, then the other. 'Your head feel OK?' The ambulance man asked. Ben nodded; held his breath as he felt the woman moving the towel around his leg.

'No concussion, by the look of it, mate.' The man glanced towards Ben's stump, then back at him. 'You've given yourself a decent whack there, though. Don't panic — blood always looks worse than it really is. We'll get you to hospital, and they can take a good look at you.'

The woman was at the ambulance, unloading something from the back. Ben glimpsed a stretcher. *It's like last time*, he knew, *when they brought me down from the mountain. And it's all because of me. I've ruined everything.*

More pain. He cried out, and his mother's hand cupped his face. 'You all right to drive?' The ambulance officer was asking her. 'You can follow us to the hospital. Park anywhere by A&E.' Mrs Coles said something, and the woman turned to Ben.

'We're going to lift you onto the stretcher, Ben. Try to relax; it'll take only a second.' To his mum, she went, 'Can you hold the stump? Just support it gently; make sure it doesn't knock against anything.'

Hands slid underneath him. 'Count of three,' The woman murmured. Ben gritted his teeth as he waited for the pain to rip at him again. 'One — two — three.' He rose smoothly, up then sideways. There was one stab from his leg; then he was on the stretcher, an orange blanket over him.

Another ten seconds, and he was inside the ambulance. His mother, face white and fearful, stood watching. There was blood all down the front of her shirt. His blood. Mrs Tully stood with an arm around her, staring. The ambulance man climbed into the back, next to him. 'You'll be fine, buddy. Sophie here —' he nodded towards the driver's seat 'races go-karts in her spare time, so you'll be *really* fine.'

Ben tried to smile; tried to call 'Sorry, Mum' to his mother. But more pain gouged at him, and by the time it passed, the ambulance's doors were closed, and it was backing out onto the road. The siren began its wailing again; then they were speeding towards the hospital.

THIRTY-THREE

The ambulance guy was asking him something. 'How long since the amputation, buddy?' Ben tried to think. 'About . . . six weeks? Bit more, maybe.' He heard his voice jerking; tried to speak more calmly. 'What's it — Have I —'

'You've given it a fair old belt. Must have hit the edge of the concrete. The artificial leg — prosthesis? That what you call it? — looks like it tore a chunk out of your stump when it came away. We've got it in the front, by the way. They'll know what to do when we arrive. Not long now. Try to relax.'

It was just like being taken off the mountain, all right. Except this time he knew what had happened; knew he'd made it happen. *Don't let me lose more of the leg*, he was begging inside his head. *Please don't* — he grunted as his stump flooded with pain again. 'Almost there, buddy,' The ambulance man went.

They slowed; swung under a canopy, came to a stop with the siren dying away. Almost instantly, the back doors were pulled open, and hands began easing the stretcher out. More faces were around him. He stared for a second at a fair-haired woman. Wasn't she the one from last time who . . . He couldn't tell.

Quickly but carefully, he was wheeled inside. The ambulance crew had vanished; blue uniforms were there instead. Faces looked down at him; hands pushed him along a corridor, into a room with a bright light that seemed to fill half the ceiling. A young woman appeared above him: black hair and dark eyes. Hom? No.

'Hello, Ben is it? I'm Doctor Li. Let's have a look at you. I'm going to take the towel off your stump. Good idea, to wrap it round like that. I'll pour some warm water over it, so it comes away more easily. Only be a few seconds.'

Someone passed her a metal dish, and he felt warmth seeping around his knee and calf. There was one tug which made breath hiss between his teeth; then the doctor was speaking to him again.

'Looks like you've torn away a sizeable piece of tissue.

You were wearing the prosthesis when it happened, that right?' Ben managed a nod, and Dr Li went on. 'The wound seems clean, but I'm going to wash it with a sterile solution just in case. Then I'll be putting some stitches in. And we'll wheel you into X-ray for a quick look at the area just above your stump. Don't think there's any damage to the bones, but I'd like to make sure. That OK with you?'

'Yeah,' Ben mumbled. Then: 'Sorry. I was being stupid.'

'It happens.' The doctor was bent over his torn stump. Ben felt more warmth and wetness as her hands patted and rinsed around it. 'Can you feel this?' She began pinching lightly on the skin above the amputation site. When Ben nodded, so did she. 'Good. No obvious nerve damage. We'll check again later. Now, some local anaesthetic before I put the stitches in. Just a little prick.'

There was a tiny jab at the front of his leg, another behind, on the remains of his calf, then the tug of stitches. *You idiot*, Ben told himself. *You stupid dick. Everything was going well; then you stuffed up. Yes — you.*

'All finished,' Dr Li told him. 'That's a nasty scrape on the palm of your hand there. When you landed on the concrete, I suppose. We got something for that, Jake?'

Ben jerked at the name. Next moment, another head appeared beside the doctor's. A big, shaven head. 'Hey, buddy,' Jake said. 'You trying to get extra sessions with my big bro, or something? Must be an easier way.'

Soothing ointment was spread over his palm. Jake wound a dressing around that, while Dr Li fixed another over his stump. He was wheeled into X-ray, where a machine clicked and murmured over his damaged leg for a few seconds, then out again. A couple of minutes, and the doctor was beside him once more.

'Good news. No bones broken. We're going to keep you in here overnight; make sure there's no more bleeding. Mr Dev will have a look at you in the morning. He can tell you more.'

Mr Dev. How angry would the surgeon be? What could Ben say to him? Maddie, too: would he ever get the chance to say *anything* to her? Another stuff-up he'd made.

And, more than anything else just now, what was going to happen to the rest of his maimed leg?

He'd just been helped into bed, a protective cradle over his stump like last time, when his parents came in. His mother had changed her top, Ben saw.

'How are you feeling, son?' his dad asked. Mrs Coles

said nothing; instead she took his unbandaged hand and held it between both of hers.

'I'm OK,' Ben told them. 'Mum, Dad, I'm sorry. It was my fault. I was a total idiot.'

His mother pressed his hand; still said nothing. His father gave a little shrug. 'Main thing is you're all right, mate. Looks like you'll be off that new leg for a while, though. Fourteen stitches, that young doctor told us. And she says they've sent the leg off to your prosthetist, but it looks pretty wrecked.'

'Is it hurting, love?' His mum spoke for the first time since she'd arrived.

'Just a bit. Serves me right.' *And there's no phantom pain*, he suddenly thought. *The real one must have scared it away.*

'Don't be too hard on yourself, buddy,' his father said then. 'We know how much you wanted to be out with your mates. Yeah, you made a silly mistake. Big thing now is not to make it again.'

'Anyway,' his mum went, 'let's see what Mr Dev has to say in the morning. He'll know if . . .' Her voice trailed away.

After his parents left, half an hour later, Ben lay and stared at the ceiling. Amazing how adults could talk such good sense sometimes. But . . . his mother's words at the end: what sort of awful things might Mr Dev have to tell him?

He had some dinner, but didn't eat much. His leg hurt — a lot, much more than he'd told his parents. He lay there, promising himself that he'd do things differently this time. He'd have to start again; he knew: wheelchair and crutches like before. He'd do it all properly. He'd take things slowly.

But all the time, one thought beat in his mind. How badly had he injured the stump? When he saw Mr Dev, would the surgeon say that more of his leg had to go? Would he . . . would he have to lose still more of his maimed leg?

THIRTY-FOUR

He hardly slept. The new wound stabbed and throbbed. Twice, a uniformed figure stood by the bed, taking his pulse. Once, a voice asked if he was hurting; did he want any pain relief? Ben mumbled 'No'. Maybe if he let himself suffer now, somehow that would mean Mr Dev didn't have to do any more. Stupid, stupid . . .

He slid into a doze near morning; woke to hear feet moving and trolleys rattling in the corridor. A bit later, a smiling Pasifika nurse came in — the same one from the first time he'd been in here. She — Lagi — looked at the chart by his bed. 'Mālō, Ben. No breakfast for you till the doctor has been, sorry. But we won't forget you, promise. I'll be back if you're allowed to eat.'

Ben swallowed. No breakfast. That must mean he'd be needing an operation. And that meant his leg was . . .

He tried breathing deep and slow, like they'd taught him after the last time. He struggled to think things out. How much more of his leg might he lose? What things might he never be able to do? Would he even be able to wear another prosthetic leg? If only he'd waited and been sensible . . .

More footsteps, two pairs of them. Then Mr Dev was in the room, a woman nurse following him, and gazing down at Ben.

'Well, young man.' The surgeon's face looked serious. 'We meet again.'

'I'm sorry.' Ben had said the words to so many people in the last hours. Now they came tumbling out again. 'I was stupid. It's all my fault.'

Mr Dev had already turned back the bed sheets and was undoing the dressing around Ben's stump. The nurse passed him a pair of scissors.

'You had a fall, I hear.' The surgeon handed a crumpled dressing to the nurse, then bent to look closely at the new wound.

'It was my fault.' (*Can't you say something . . . original?* Ben's mind was asking.)

'Well, that's why we tell you not to rush into things. You've been handling things well so far. Pity you've had this setback.'

The surgeon was still studying the new wound. 'Now, there's quite an area of tissue been torn here, but Dr Li's done a very nice job. You won't have to put up with any more stitches from me.'

Ben's breath caught. He swallowed; made himself speak. 'Mr Dev? Do — do you need to take any more of my leg off?'

The surgeon was fixing a new dressing to the stump. He glanced at Ben; looked surprised. 'No, no. You'll have to use a wheelchair till the new scar heals, like you did before. And I hear you're going to need another prosthesis. You'd better do some apologising to Tim. But no — your leg will stay exactly as it is, don't worry.'

Ben heard himself make another sound. It wasn't a question, this time. It was a choking noise. The noise someone makes just before they start crying.

He had four more visitors before his parents arrived

mid-morning. The nurse Lagi appeared again, smiling even more. 'Good news, I hear. So what would you like for breakfast? Sausages or bacon or hash browns or eggs? Oh, I forgot — you're a teenage boy. Would you like *all* of them?'

In fact, he didn't eat much. He still felt too churned up, though this time it was from relief, not fear.

He'd finished; was sitting propped up in bed, looking down at the cradle protecting his residual leg from the bed sheets, just like one had those six . . . seven weeks back, when a small stocky figure strode in. Tim looked at Ben and shook his shaven head. 'What's your problem, mate? Don't you like my brilliant work? You wanna get yourself a different panel beater?'

Ben didn't answer for a second. He was staring at Tim's right ear. Then he mumbled, 'Sorry. It was all my fault.' Maybe he should get those words tattooed on his forehead?

'Ah, you're not the first. You young guys are always in a tearing hurry to be up and doing again. Anyway, socket area's fairly stuffed, but the foot looks OK, and that's the most expensive bit. Actually, it's made me realise I might need to make the socket deeper, so I'd probably have had to do that anyway. I don't usually ask for a test drive like yours to find out, though.'

He glanced at his watch. 'So I'll see you — again — in a few weeks. You know the routine now, anyhow. I'll tell you one thing, though, buddy. You stuff this next leg up, and I won't be using the lipstick on the socket. I'll shove it up your nose instead.'

The prosthetist grinned at Ben, began turning away, then saw Ben staring again. He sighed and touched his right ear. It was swollen and bruised. 'Yes, I've been playing more squash. Not with Mr Dev, though. This was from Hom. I've been teaching her a few shots. I tell you, mate — physios are even more lethal than surgeons.'

He had a text from Manu. *Hey, bro. U r useless if we don't keep an eye on u. C U when u r home. Miriana sez hi.*

Ben had just answered it, and another from Connor (*Heard of shaking a leg, but u r crazy!*), when he heard a voice in the corridor nearby. It seemed to be asking a question. Ben went still. He knew that voice! Feet approached his room, and Maddie Yelich appeared. Her face looks different, too, was Ben's first thought. Not like Tim's, but . . .

'Hey,' she went. Ben said 'Hey' back, and she stood gazing at the protective cradle over his leg. 'You all right?' The girl asked, then shook her head before he could answer. 'Sorry. Silly question.'

'Nah. Yeah, I'm all right. I'm stupid, though. It was my fault; I stuffed up completely.' *I better get that tattoo*, he decided.

'What happened, exactly?' she asked. Ben told her. Being in a bad mood (he didn't say it was partly because he thought he might not see her again). Having a row with his mother. Stamping out the door onto the steps. Falling.

Maddie kept watching him. She shook her head again when he finished. 'That is such a . . . such a *not clever* thing to do!'

They both laughed, and Ben's whole body seemed to grow lighter. 'You in to see Tessa?' he asked.

'Yeah. Your mum told mine that you were here. Some people just can't stay away.' The girl was silent, then: 'My last check-up with her for a while. Hand's working really well, so I don't need to come back for three months, then maybe just twice a year, like I've done before, till this one gets too small.'

Neither of them said anything for a few moments. *She looks different, somehow*, Ben thought again. He couldn't decide how. Or how he felt about her not coming to the hospital anymore.

'You seen Angus?' he asked.

Maddie Yelich made a gulping noise. 'He's — he's dead.' Then it was her turn to cry.

THIRTY-FIVE

A heart attack, she told him, when she'd stopped weeping, grabbed some tissues from the box beside Ben's bed, and blown her nose. She'd flopped down into one of the chairs and sat staring at the floor. 'He hadn't been feeling well for a while. Tessa asked him about it; told him to go see his GP. But Angus said . . . he didn't want to bother anyone.' She used another couple of tissues. 'He collapsed and died in his flat Monday afternoon. Just after — just after he'd got back from the hospital.'

Ben remembered the old bloke hunched over his walking stick in the waiting room, the way he'd staggered when he stood up that time. He gazed at the bed sheets. Maddie wiped her cheeks. The hospital was going to have to buy more tissues. 'Mum and I are going to his funeral tomorrow. Tessa's probably coming, too.'

'He was such a cool old guy,' Ben said again.

The girl nodded. 'I liked him heaps. Remember how he called us lassie and laddie?'

'Yeah. And saying that we — we can do anything. That was amazing.'

Maddie was still looking at the floor. 'When he was going out of the waiting room — when he stopped and said "Be kind" to us?' She raised her head and gazed at Ben. 'It was almost like he knew what was going to happen.'

Neither of them spoke for a while. Then Ben asked, 'Can — can you let me know how the funeral goes?'

'OK. I'll give you a ring tomorrow, maybe? Oh —' she half-smiled. 'My mum's meeting your mum for coffee. Turns out they went to the same primary school. So they keep remembering all sorts of stuff.'

After another moment, Maddie stood. 'I better be going. Mum'll be thinking I've got lost. Hey — don't be such a clever boy this time, eh? Don't go ru—'

'— Don't go rushing into things,' Ben said before she could, and they both laughed again.

'See ya,' she said.

'Yeah,' he replied. 'See ya.' Inside his head, he added, *Hope so.*

He lay and thought about Angus. *When I'm really old, say fifty or even sixty, I wouldn't mind being like that*, he decided. Travel the world, have an interesting job. Not let what's happened stop me. And . . . yeah, be kind to people, like Angus had said.

And he thought about himself. What he used to be, before that day on Pangonui. What he was now, and would be for the rest of his life. He'd started facing up to it before; now he had to accept that he'd never be absolutely the same person again. There were ways in which he was changed forever. But that happened to everyone as they grew up, and grew older, anyway. And he was going to make sure he did absolutely everything he could — plus a bit extra. He wasn't just going to give things his best shot. He was going to give them his best-and-more shot.

So for quarter of an hour, sitting there in the hospital bed, he went through as many of his physio exercises as he could. The deep breathing. The arm-swinging and leg-raising (his own, right leg only, just now). The bum-clenching. No way was he ever, ever going to tell *anyone* about the bum-clenching.

He was just finishing the arm-swinging when his fourth visitor, Dr Li, came in with a nurse. Jake? Not unless Jake had shrunk 20 centimetres and grown dreadlocks. The young doctor smiled. 'You look like you're ready to be up and doing. I'll just check those stitches and then we'll send you on your way.'

'I know Mr Dev has already had a look,' she went on as she bent over his left leg. 'But hospitals love being fussy.' The scissors and the gentle tug of dressings. The dreadlocked nurse left the room. 'Looking good. No sign of infection,' The doctor said. 'I've used stitches that'll dissolve by themselves in five or six days, but get your parents to make an appointment with your GP for a final check.' Another smile. 'And I believe you've already had lessons on how to take care of the stump?'

Ben's face went warm, but he nodded. 'Yeah. Thanks, Dr Li.' He started to say something about 'my fault', but his brain went *bo-ring!*, so he changed it to 'I'll be sensible this time'.

The doctor laughed as she reached for a fresh dressing. 'Wonderful to hear a teenager say that.' She turned as a rumbling sound came from the doorway, and the nurse with dreadlocks returned, pushing a wheelchair. 'Oh, and I believe you know how to use one of these as well?'

He got dressed by himself, easing his clothes on carefully

over the bandaged stump. The left leg of his jeans would have to hang down till he got home and his mum pinned it up. No, he'd learn to pin it up himself. About time he did.

His parents arrived just ten minutes later; stared at Ben sitting on the edge of the bed, doing still more arm-swings. They both broke into smiles. His mother kissed him on the cheek; his father rested a hand on his shoulder. 'Well, matey,' he said. 'Here we go again.'

'Yeah.' Then Ben gazed at each of them in turn. 'Mum, Dad, I'm sorry, OK?' His parents both began to speak, but he shook his head, and they stopped. *Power!* Ben thought. 'I stuffed up. I rushed into things.' (Maybe he should have that tattooed on his forehead as well?) 'And you guys have done so much for me. I know that. So I promise: I'm going to do everything the best I can from now on. And I'm gonna be careful, take my time about doing things, like everyone kept telling me to. I'll listen to them, and to you. OK, end of speech.'

His mother was smiling, though there were tears in her eyes. *How* does *she manage to do that?* Ben wondered. Mr Coles laughed. 'Should have made a recording of that. Great stuff, son. You can do it; we know that.'

'Dr Li says you can come home right now — unless you feel like staying for a bit?' He laughed again at Ben's expression; then he pushed the wheelchair up to the bed. 'Ever seen one of these before?'

Sounds like Dr Li's joke, Ben thought. *There must be another school, where adults all learn to make them.* He began easing himself off the bed. When his mother stepped forward to help, he opened his mouth to tell her he could manage by himself, then shut it.

Then the three of them left the hospital room, to start all over again.

THIRTY-SIX

The days grew shorter. Then for month after month, they got longer, till they began to shorten once more.

Ben was so used to his second prosthesis by now, he sometimes almost forgot he was wearing it. Most days, he could put it on and take it off without even looking. But there were still moments when he found himself gazing down at his left leg, remembering when it was his own skin and bone, when he could do anything with it. And there were still moments when he grieved for the loss of it.

Sometimes, he needed his stick. But mostly, he could walk without it. A few times, he deliberately left it at home if he wasn't going to be doing much. A few other times, he forgot it. On those days, he asked for help if he needed to. He'd learned to do that, too.

Stairs were still tricky. Escalators were even more tricky. He couldn't turn around really quickly if his weight was on the left leg. But the phantom pains and itches in his missing limb didn't come so often now, or maybe he'd got used to them as well.

Hom came to see him twice a week, then once a week, once a fortnight, and finally only once a month. Both she and Tim told him he'd done brilliantly — 'this time'. Ben thought of his physio and prosthetist together, because they'd both helped so much. And because one time, when he'd had an appointment with Tim, he'd found Hom sitting there with the shaven-headed figure, the two of them talking quietly — and holding hands. Hom got up to go, gave Tim a kiss on the cheek, told Ben, 'You do not see that.' The prosthetist pointed a finger at Ben. 'You tell people, I'll be after you with the lipstick!'

He had met Mr Dev, too, in the hospital corridor one Wednesday. The surgeon watched as Ben walked steadily towards him, with his stick. 'Well done,' he smiled. 'And I hope I *don't* see you again!'

He kept remembering Angus's words, how kids could do anything. He believed that, now. Believed also that being careful meant he could do more of those things. There'd been a few times when he thought that if one more person said 'Remember: don't rush into . . .', he'd kick them with his new prosthesis. But he'd learned to handle that, too.

Anyway, it was so brilliant being ordinary again. His parents had even told him off for not tidying his room. Great!

At school, he was just like the rest of the students. He'd whistled and cheered and stamped (both feet; his prosthesis made a good loud noise) when Connor won the school talent quest with his own song — not about Ben. Phew!

Girls had stopped fussing over him a long time back. A couple of times, he'd bumped into somebody in the corridor, and they'd gone 'Watch where you're going, can't you?', before they realised, and looked embarrassed.

His English and Social Studies were going fine. He was managing in Maths and Science, too, though he'd never be as good as Manu. Soccer? That was a dream from his life before everything changed. But he didn't mind now. 'Hey, when you turn pro, I'll be your manager,' he told Manu one day. 'I'll charge you a special low rate — a million bucks a year.'

Once or twice at home, when he was hopping around after he'd washed the prosthesis, he caught his mum looking at his stump and saw the sadness on her face. Yeah, other people still grieved as well.

And he'd still give almost anything to have his real leg back. He guessed he'd always feel like that. But he knew he was a different guy now, because of what had happened. He'd grown up, in some ways.

There were a couple of times he'd never forget. He woke in the night once; knew he needed to go to the loo. He pulled himself out of bed, yawning and half-asleep, and set off. Next moment, he was collapsing sideways, grabbing at the duvet, sliding down to thump onto his bum on the floor. He'd completely forgotten about his missing leg. He sprawled there for a bit, and realised he was trying not to laugh. What a dick! Luckily, his parents hadn't heard.

Then there was the Saturday, four . . . five months after he'd fallen on the back step. He'd gone to watch Connor and Manu's soccer team play, and he'd been standing on the sideline, feeling pretty down suddenly that he'd never play again.

Halfway through the second half, someone on his mates' team hurt an ankle. There were no reserves, so they were down to ten players. Ben heard a voice say 'I'll go goalie', and swallowed as he realised it was his. He walked onto the field, while everyone stared.

A few minutes later, the other team were given a penalty. 'Let Manu be goalie for this', a couple of voices called, but Manu said, 'Nah, Ben'll do it. You show them, bro.'

So he stood on the goal line, facing the kicker. Before the boy started to run in, his eyes flicked towards the left side of the net. As boot met ball, Ben stepped across in that direction, flung out an arm, punched the ball away. Next second, hands were thumping him on the back, shouting 'Awesome, Ben! Brilliant!' He couldn't stop grinning for hours.

A few times, little kids at the shops or in the street wanted to know what had happened to him, and did it hurt? Their parents looked awkward, but Ben didn't mind answering. 'I kept biting my toenails,' he told the kids. 'Nah — a boulder fell on me, because I was silly.' Then he always said, 'So you be careful. Give things your best shot, but don't rush into it.' It felt cool saying that last part to others.

Now he and Maddie Yelich stood on the shingle slopes of Pangonui. Their mothers were back in the carpark, five minutes' walk below, getting the picnic ready. Mr Coles had just caught up to boy and girl with the phone he'd left in the car.

Ben leaned on his stick; gazed towards the group of boulders he'd last seen nearly eight months ago. No wind today, but he wore a parka. He was trying to stay sensible about stuff like that, too.

Beside him, Maddie ('She's cool, eh?' Manu said after he met her. Connor went, 'Yeah, so how come she's interested in Ben?') was looking in the same direction. She wore her red mitten today, to protect her prosthetic hand from any gravel and rocks.

'That where it happened?' she asked.

Ben nodded. The boulder that had changed his life lay on the slope, just below the huge ones. It looked smaller than he remembered. All he'd been worrying about then was his teeth — were his good looks going to be ruined for ever? (*OK, what good looks?*)

Maddie stared across the shingle slope, at the tall stand of bush rising on the far side, the green and gold lichen on boulders, the way the mountain angled up till its peak vanished in drifting clouds. 'This is so awesome! Angus would have really liked seeing this.'

She turned to Ben. 'You nervous?'

He started to say no, then went, 'A bit. But I'm not gonna push it too far. I just wanted to be back here. It's such an amazing place.'

'Amazing that you can be here, too, eh?'

Ben nodded. His father had arrived behind them, phone in hand. 'All right, buddy. This is what you've been waiting for. But like we agreed — just partway across, then back.'

Maddie grinned. 'I'll look after him, Mr Coles.'

'Someone has to. And you look after Maddie, mate. She's never been up here before, remember?' Then Ben's father stepped forward, put his arms around his son, and held him. 'I'll be right behind you. Get going, then, or your mothers will have eaten all the picnic.'

I'm gonna be sore after this, Ben knew. *It doesn't matter.* He gazed around, too, for a second. Maddie was right: this was awesome. Just like the other awesome things he was going to do in his life.

'Ready?' he asked her and gripped his stick. He blinked

as she slipped her hand into his free one. Her real hand: it felt warm and smooth against his. He glanced at her; she glanced at him; both of them looked away.

Then the ordinary, extraordinary pair of them started off across the shingle slope.

Caught in a tunnel collapse, Liam and Imogen have to use all their wits to survive in this gripping novel for readers eight years and up.

> *When you stood deep inside the tunnel, you could hear the mountain groaning overhead. That's what Liam Geary's father had told him, anyway. It sounded stupid, till you stood inside a big tunnel; felt those billions of tonnes pressing in from above and the sides; heard water dripping from ceilings, or even trickling like something's blood behind the concrete walls; sensed the blackness that lay beyond the TBM's blazing lights as it ground its slow way through the stone ahead. Then you knew that a major tunnel like the Puketapu was a place of power, somehow; that darkness and danger lurked all around.*

When Liam dares his classmate Imogen to come on a forbidden tour of the railway tunnel being drilled through a nearby mountain, he hopes she'll quit protesting about it damaging the environment — his dad is an engineer working on the tunnel, after all.

Just as they reach the huge tunnelling machine everything goes horribly wrong. When the rocks stop falling and the dust settles, they are trapped, kilometres below ground, in the dark. Water is trickling in and beginning to rise. And nobody knows where they are.

Can they stop arguing and start working together to escape before time runs out?

Wright Family Foundation Esther Glen Award for Junior Fiction 2023
Also available as an ebook

Funny, moving and devastatingly honest, *See Ya, Simon* is a New Zealand favourite that has won several awards and has been translated into seven languages. A must read for all teenagers.

Simon is a typical teenager — in every way except one. Simon likes girls, weekends and enjoys mucking about and playing practical jokes. But what is different is that Simon has muscular dystrophy — he is in a wheelchair and doesn't have long to live. *See Ya, Simon* is told by Simon's best friend, Nathan. Funny, moving and devastatingly honest, it tells of their last year together.

Winner of the Times Educational Supplement Nasen Award, the Silver Pen Award and the Storylines Gaelyn Gordon Award for a Much-loved Book, *See Ya, Simon* has been published in the USA, UK, Germany, Denmark, the Netherlands, China, Japan and Slovenia.

Also available as an ebook